HOW A MAN

FACES

ADVERSITY

LifeSkills for Men

How a Man Faces Adversity, Robert Hicks
How a Man Handles Conflict at Work, Paul Tomlinson
How a Man Prepares His Daughters for Life, Michael Farris
How a Man Prepares His Sons for Life, Michael O'Donnell
How a Man Prays for His Family, John Yates
How a Man Stands Up for Christ, Jim Gilbert

Also of Interest

How to Build a Life-Changing Men's Ministry,
Steve Sonderman

9604

LIFESKILLS
FOR MEN

HOW A MAN FACES ADVERSITY

ROBERT HICKS

DAVID HAZARD, *General Editor*

BETHANY HOUSE PUBLISHERS
MINNEAPOLIS, MINNESOTA 55438

How a Man Faces Adversity
Copyright © 1996
Robert Hicks

Published by Bethany House Publishers
A Ministry of Bethany Fellowship, Inc.
11300 Hampshire Avenue South
Minneapolis, Minnesota 55438

Printed in the United States of America.

Library of Congress Cataloging-in-Publication Data

CIP applied for

ISBN 1–55661–847–6   CIP

To the faculty of Seminary of the East

A blessed band of brothers and sisters
who have always stood by me in adversity,
colleagues beyond the pale.

Dr. Robert Hicks is the bestselling author of *Uneasy Manhood* and *The Masculine Journey*. His career has included pastoring, counseling, and military chaplaincy. Hicks is Professor of Pastoral Theology at Seminary of the East.

Contents

Preface 9
1. Men and Adversity 15
2. Taken by Surprise 25
3. Out of Control 37
4. Unhealthy Ways Men Deal With Adversity 51
5. Enemies That Defeat Us From Within 69
6. God's View of Adversity and Ours 87
7. How God Looks Upon Adversity:
   Light in the Midst of Darkness 99
8. CHRIST . . . Who Suffers With Us 111
9. Attacking Adversity 123

Preface

"A brother is born for adversity."

Proverbs 17:17

ad-ver-si-ty 1: a condition of suffering, destitution, or affliction 2: a calamitous or disastrous experience[1]

Jon knew the political climate had changed, but being a civil servant held certain protections. He couldn't be fired without criminal charges being filed on him. Though he worked for an elected official, we all thought our friend was "safe" and would survive any change of administration. How naive we were. In an instant, Jon went from prominent government official to fighting for his very life and reputation. His new boss trumped up criminal charges, and he was out, having to spend all his time defending his twenty years of public service. A small cadre of Christian brothers, including me, promised that we would stand by Jon whether he was found guilty or not. An even greater stretch was that we would be brothers to him even if he was guilty of wrongdoing no matter how the verdict came out. After all, aren't brothers born for adversity?

Adversity means life has turned against us. Adversity is a mud slide of bad circumstances. It's an experience of having the forces of life turned against us. This definition then presupposes better times and better fortunes. It's not a "good news"/"bad news" joke, and there is no option to hear the good news first. There *is* no good news, and the bad news, unfortunately, is no joke.

If you just picked up this book and have read this far, let me enlighten you a little about the contents of the volume. When I was asked to write this book, I humorously thought to myself it could be very short. A very short book indeed . . . only three words. How *do* men face adversity? *Not very well!*

Oh, sure, men go off to battle, train to be in special forces, endure severe hardships, play football, and navigate in and out of traffic jams without falling apart. Some call these things *adversity*. But these are the kinds of things we men do for fun, work, or just plain showing off to other guys or some attractive female in the next lane. These kinds of "adversities" are mostly under our control and a part of our decision-making processes. A sort of typical show of masculine prowess which adds to the impression that we can do just about anything. We can *handle* these experiences because they are to some extent under our control. But life is not like the male pastime of TV-channel surfing. When adversity strikes, we do not have the option of changing the channel. We can point the remote in the direction of the overwhelming circumstance, but it doesn't go away. And with it, a pain invades our lives and stays, and to some extent must be dealt with. At least acknowledged. That leads to the question: How do we as men deal with pain? From my years as a pastor, counselor, seminary professor, and military chaplain I have to say, "Not very well *at all*."

Men try to handle adversity with a certain primal propensity. We shield ourselves, blunting the next oncoming punch, just waiting for a chance to strike out and land one. . . . Revenge! That's how most of us try to thwart or stand against the pain of adversity. After all, a male with any testosterone left in his body would not respond in any other way, would he? Real men don't "learn from" adversity, or "welcome" it—they *fight* it!

What's worse, no one has ever prepared us for the bully blows and adversities that life throws our way. I know my own father faced great adversities in his life—a poor upbringing, not much education, tuberculosis, job downsizings, and, of course, raising me! But he never allowed me the privilege of gaining a glimpse of insight into his soul about these matters. In his day, there must have been a sort of masculine contract made and signed by all men not to ever discuss their pain with their sons. I appreciate the fact that he never burdened me with his problems, but as a man standing in mid-life, I now wish I would have had a little preparation for the painful realities of life. No, most fathers don't prepare their sons for such things. I am not sure we really can—but it is possible to let them know that adversity is a normal part of life. And to expect it.

Likewise, in my educational trek I missed the crucial course labeled Adversity 101. If it was there, it must have been an elective or carefully hidden somewhere in the curriculum. (It was between Qualitative and Quantitative Analysis, two other courses I stayed away from like the plague.) Education does not exactly prepare men for adversity, unless you are Attention Deficit Disordered or hyperactive and spend most of your time in the principal's office.

And then there's the church. Which one, I'm not sure.

They all seem to be variations on the same theme when it comes to adversity. But in my experience, we tell our people to be "good soldiers of Jesus Christ" (2 Timothy 2:3), sing "Onward Christian Soldiers," and too often shoot our best warriors in the back. When they come back bleeding, we ask, "Why are you bleeding, is there something wrong with you?" Brilliant, we acknowledge that life is warfare and then are surprised when someone gets wounded, often by our own bullets! I wonder how many wounded men are currently sitting in our church pews, bruised and still bleeding from unacknowledged adversity. I also wonder how many of these, when they finally open up and acknowledge their wounds, will find only blame and shame from their "comforters." In some circles we men have elevated blaming the victim to an art form. It's so easy to find reasons to not truly honor the struggles of our brothers, thus compounding their adversity.

So to this one man, and to many other men I know, it seems men don't handle adversity well. Statistics confirm my intestinal hunch. Some believe men are the favored gender. The reality is men show higher rates of criminal activity, suicide, childhood emotional disorders, alcoholism, drug addiction—and, of course, a shorter life-span than our feminine counterparts.[2] I can't conclusively prove that these statistics are the long-term results of men who have never dealt appropriately with the adversity in their lives. But I do know from my own counseling experience, and my work in the field of posttraumatic stress studies, that much of what we call mental or emotional illness is, in fact, the result of an unsatisfactory attempt to deal with tragedy or traumatic events. So how one faces adversity may have profound impact upon the rest of a man's life.

This being the case, I welcome women into this book, too. For women, I write as one trying to give insight into the male mystique on the subject of pain and how men deal with it. Women often see a man's pain before he is aware of it himself. There are reasons for this, but the reality of the differences between us is an important one. Knowing the dynamics and tendencies of the way a male processes his thoughts and feelings can give women and wives a heads up in understanding the men in their lives.

For my male readers, I write as a fellow-traveler and brother-in-arms . . . one, who having been wounded, is trying to carry the more critically injured back to safety. In this sense, the book is spiritual buddy care, the first echelon of healing. I hope both my feminine and masculine readers can sense the spirit underneath my verbalizing. When adversity strikes, men often get lost in their confusion and pain. What a man needs at these times is someone to walk through the pain with him.

A story is told of a man who, having been lost in a dense forest for days, finally sat down on a log and wept uncontrollably. As he cried, the sound of someone or something coming through the brush alerted him. As he looked up, he saw another man emerge out of the thick foliage. The lost soul jumped up and wrapped his arms around his new-found friend. He uttered, "Thank God, I'm saved, now we can get out of here." The other man, wiping a tear out his own eye, replied, "I'm lost too, but I'll walk with you."

This book is one man's attempt to walk through the woods with a newfound friend. *You.* Hopefully, with God's help and our journeying together, we'll find the way out together!

Notes

1. *Webster's New Collegiate Dictionary* (Springfield, Mass.: G. & C. Merriam Co.), p. 17.
2. Herb Goldberg, *The Hazards of Being Male: Surviving the Myth of Masculine Privilege* (New York: Signet Classic, New American Library, 1976), p. 5.

1

Men and Adversity

Richard had everything going his way. He had out-hustled all the rest of his companions in the marketing department. He was named top salesmen for his Fortune 500 company by the age of twenty-nine. An attractive wife, three wonderful kids, a country club membership with the obligatory upper-middle class suburban home—it was all part of the package. For his outstanding-performer status, he won frequent trips abroad for his wife and family. The fringes and rewards were many. Meanwhile . . .

I was a poor graduate student at the time, living near the inner-city, quite a different community indeed. Therefore, I was always grateful when Richard came by my school to pick me up and take me to some fine restaurant for lunch. A free lunch then, as well as now, was always appreciated. But underneath the genuine appreciation for my friend's generosity, I was inwardly jealous. I was probably terribly jealous! Here I was, barely making it financially, paying my tuition, and putting food on the table for my expanding family, while Richard was a high-flyer.

Time and circumstances have changed my perspective. Today, Richard is wifeless, jobless, and, for all practical purposes, childless. The stressor of a company downsizing and unemployment first took its toll on his wife—then on the marriage, then on his own health. When his wife had enough, she moved out, taking the kids. Then she filed for divorce. Richard became more and more depressed and was finally hospitalized . . . in the psych-ward.

As far as I know, Richard has never really recovered. Apparently, the adversity of unemployment and divorce and being separated from his children was more than he could face. Neither his self-confidence nor his faith in God remained intact. Richard's life, I have come to realize, is not an aberration. In fact, it is more of a paradigm for how many men face adversity. Or at least try to.

Adversity is something no one really prepares for. So, when it strikes, we as men are terribly blind-sided by its impact. Some may walk through it strong and victorious. But I have observed in my many years of counseling that when men get totally honest about their trials, the stories of bewilderment, disillusionment, and a quiet, bitter res-ignation are what emerge. These responses make me some-times question the honesty of those "triumphant brothers" who seem so oblivious or impervious to feeling their pain. For most males with a 98.6 temperature, adversity causes pain. And men do not deal with pain real well!

Al was a radiant, smiling, energetic city kid. Even though he was surrounded by opportunities to make the fast buck, he was committed to walking "straight" and try-ing to improve his life. Al tried his best to defy the odds by excelling in school. His godly, churchgoing mother was also always on his heels. She monitored his homework and friends, met with his teachers, and was Al's greatest fan on the athletic fields. But in spite of all her good intentions and vigilance, and Al's commitment to the straight life, he fell into the typical inner-city wrongdoing.

After being caught with a stolen car and a controlled substance in his possession, he faced inevitable jail time. The arrest by itself shattered Al's ambition. His experience doing time was the kind of trauma young men don't ever talk about. The sexual molestation from fellow prisoners and the physical abuse from guards caused Al to throw off all the proper upbringing his mother had instilled in him. His dream of a better life was robbed because of a few dumb decisions and his inability to say no. Because he couldn't talk about the trauma, he ensured that he would not recover from it. The adversity Al went through marked him for the rest of his life. His mother still prays for him and believes he can yet get his life together.

Wayne's experience is not as extreme as Al's on the surface—but in the final analysis it had the same devastating long-term effects. Wayne was the senior pastor of a large evangelical church. All his ministerial hopes and dreams since graduating from seminary were coming together in his ministry at Oak Tree Community. He had seen the church membership grow from 500 when he first came to over 2,000 within ten years. As a result of his success, he became a regular speaker on the church growth and pastors' conferences circuit. He loved speaking at these conferences and sharing the keys to his success.

But while his expertise was being valued across the country, his board of trustees began to have serious doubts about the integrity of Wayne's own life and ministry. Certain elders had concerns about the pastor's family life and, in particular, his teenaged children. It had been brought to the attention of several of the elders that his two teenaged sons were running in the wrong crowd, and they were seldom seen in church. The "concern" became an infectious cancer among the very men who vigorously recruited Wayne to be the senior pastor.

Everything came to a head at one infamous board meeting. The board felt on the basis of 1 Timothy 3 that Wayne no longer had his household under control and should take a leave of absence from the pulpit.

In reaction and retaliation, Wayne made the mistake of revealing he had counseled several of the wives and children of elders, and if he was disqualified, most of the board should be also. The board was outraged and rebuked him, saying he had no right to divulge such confidential information in front of the entire board. His reaction became the *coup de grace* for them. His inappropriate response only confirmed their view that he was "unteachable" and no longer qualified for pastoral ministry. The board moved to require Wayne to take a leave of absence, not just from the pulpit but also from the ministry—a move they viewed as extremely gracious.

Wayne was devastated. In the months following his forced resignation, he and his wife swung through the emotional extremes of denial, rage, and depression. Finally, Wayne left the ministry discouraged, disillusioned, and depressed. To support his family, he went to work for his father-in-law. Wayne is still trying to put his life and faith back together. But it's not easy.

These three examples illustrate that in spite of all our efforts to look strong, talk strong, be strong, most of us do not deal with adversity well. In fact, current research suggests men do not deal with painful events with *any* of the same positive constitution or resources that women naturally utilize. Take any statistic and it reveals men do not do as well as women when it comes to dealing with adversity.

Consider this: 90 percent of all homeless adults are

men, 80 percent of all suicides are men (though women *attempt* it more). Besides the fact that men are more likely to work in the "death professions" (miners, construction workers, firemen, policemen, etc.), men are still *three times* more likely to be murdered than women. In 1992, 90 percent of highway fatalities were men, 82 percent of homicides were men.[1]

Even though I've been helping men through their problems for many years, I can't predict what *ought* to be traumatic or painful for any particular man. One man may survive the worst life throws at him without any adverse effects. Another man becomes totally immobilized because his lawnmower broke.

Apparently, we men have differing breaking points. What we do have in common is our own human fragility. We have inherited from our first parents a flawed human nature which accounts for differing degrees of human limitation. Under the right kind of duress, each of us will watch our most trusted strengths and virtues dissolve.

But what gives some men the stamina and patience to make it through? How do men get it together again when they feel as though they're about to crack?

This I *can* tell you up front: Adversity puts us face-to-face with the enemy of our souls. His most seasoned and accurate weapons are the "slings and arrows of outrageous fortune." Later, I will outline the various kinds of outrageous fortune men face and tell you how they can get through. But, for now, be assured that no one escapes some kind of adversity. The apostle Paul assured his readers that whatever temptation or adversity they were facing, it was common to human living. (See 1 Corinthians 10:13.)[2] Apparently, even committed Christians are not immune to feeling adrift when adversity strikes, thus calling forth the need to encourage such under trial (James 1:2).

When adversity strikes, our normal competencies and spiritual strengths can be brought down. In these moments of spiritual collapse, we encounter something devilishly new within ourselves. We may encounter a darkened person living within—a man we may not like, or even disdain. During these "dark night of the soul" experiences, we come face-to-face with a much darker side of ourselves. A darkness born, or at least revealed, through the pain of adversity.

Ken was unstoppable in his career as a journalist until his "dark night" hit. He was about to reach a top post in a large city daily newspaper when his little boy was killed. The hard-nosed reporter in him crumbled. His wife went into severe depression, and the "crack manager" in him couldn't manage her wildly spiraling emotions—let alone his own. He began to numb the pain by drinking Jack Daniels.

Les was a Green Beret in the Special Forces. He'd parachuted behind enemy lines under fire and kept his men together under extremely dangerous conditions. But this tough army commander could not "command" love and respect from his wife once the war was over. After four years of marriage, he had barked orders at her so often that she disappeared with their two small sons. Les lost control of his rage and assaulted a man in a parking lot when the guy wouldn't move his car at Les's insistence. When Les realized his career was ruined because of the criminal charge, he caved in.

A great irony, isn't it? The traits that are our greatest strengths can become our greatest enemies.

Those of us who believe in God can piously quote Romans 8:28, knowing that "God causes all things to work together for good." But this does not mean adversity will *automatically* make us a better human being or a more spiritually minded person. The man who sits around waiting for God to turn straw into gold is missing the opportunity—and the challenge—to grow.

Adversity merely reveals who we are and then asks us what we are going to do with this new insight into ourselves. Experientially, each trial makes its own unique contribution to the composite history and quality of our life. Adversity—*if* you know how to walk through it successfully—is always developmental. It doesn't leave us where it found us. It either stimulates further healthy growth or causes a demolition of the soul, resulting in spiritual strangulation or passive stagnation. Most men know the value of pumping iron and working hard. But when it comes to weighty matters of the soul or of the emotions, we can't see the value of "working out" the negative feelings which burn inside.

The enemy of our souls has quivered many sharpened arrows of misfortune for the male believer. One arrow may strike deep into one man but may miss another. But the arrows are launched in our direction nevertheless. Sooner if not later, one of these strikes the best of men and creates havoc within his life. No doubt, that's what brought you to this book.

In the next chapter, we'll explore some of the more common arrows which strike deep and traumatize the hearts of men. But before we go on, I want to encourage you: Adversity does not need to destroy your life or leave you miserable forever. As former Iranian hostage Bruce Laingen said, "We're like tea bags. We don't know our own strength until we get into hot water."

What makes the difference here is a secret revealed in one of the most leading-edge areas of study today—that is, trauma survival. In the past, mental health professionals worked on the unproven assumption that adversity and trauma would inevitably lead to future difficulty. In short, a major blow would leave you "emotionally crippled" for good. What's being discovered today is that both men and women have capacities for conquering life crises that are often hidden from them and need to be tapped. Even out of the worst situations—like the Nazi Holocaust—many survivors rebuild their lives in ways that defy logic. The findings of a recent study reports a "magnificent ability of human beings to rebuild shattered lives, careers, and families, even as they wrestle with the bitterest of memories."[3]

In a later chapter I will focus our attention on what we have learned from these survivors and what kind of resources they utilized to cope with the pain of severe crisis.

For now, let's explore the kinds of crises we men are going through.

For Thought and Discussion

1. Which man's experience in this chapter do you identify with the most? Why?
2. What strength have you always taken pride in? Can you see how it may also contribute to weakness under adverse conditions?
3. Are you consciously fighting to keep some "dark night" experience from ever getting to the surface of your life?

Notes

1. Statistics quoted in *A Man's World: How Real Is Male Privilege—and How High Is Its Price?* (New York: HarperCollins, 1995), Chapter 1, "Man as Victim," pp. 27–50.

2. The word translated "temptation," *peirasmos*, also means "trial, or test," hence, adversity.
3. Quoted in Julius Segal, *Winning Life's Toughest Battles* (New York: McGraw, 1986), p. 9.

Taken by Surprise

What makes adversity so "outrageous" is the unexpectedness and *out-of-the-blueness* with which the event strikes us. These intruders take us by surprise and rip open our emotional gut, exposing our worst fears . . . and flaws.

Bill and his wife had always had problems, but he never thought she would just up and walk out. After all, he was her sole source of financial support. However, the pain of her walking out unexpectedly compounded when he learned she had left him to be with his business partner. The double surprise was more than he could take.

Walt felt he'd been kicked in the gut when the oncologist spilled the news: "I'm sorry, but your son has an aggressive form of cancer." Inside he thought to himself, *This can't be, there must be a mistake.* In a moment, a few words from a physician had out-of-the-blue changed his life.

When Cary left home to fly to the company headquarters, he anticipated a commendation and a well-deserved raise—only to find a major corporate overhaul meant his whole department was being phased out. Instead of carrying home a sizeable bonus check to his celebrating wife, the infamous pink slip was stuffed in his coat pocket. The sudden reversal of fortune made for an agonizingly long flight home.

When Lou learned that his daughter had been sexually molested, he was ready to buy a gun and take revenge into his own hands. But when he finally learned who the perpetrator was, rage turned into utter dismay. The offender was the youth pastor of his own church. Even worse, the church leadership decided to smooth over the issue and support the youth pastor as innocent. As it turned out, the pastor and the entire church turned against Lou and his daughter, as if they were the guilty parties for making the accusation. How could someone accuse a "man of God" of such things? With all his Christian friends against him, Lou felt alone and devastated. As a father he had to deal with the pain in his daughter while trying to make sense of his own pain.

I'm Okay . . . Really

Each of these men had their own way of initially coping with the crisis they faced. Outwardly, each carried on and seemed to be "okay." But, in fact, they only internalized their trauma and refused to feel their self-pity, vengeful rage, and abandonment by God. The unexpected "out of sync" nature of these adversities threw each man into temporary shutdowns and even longer-term emotional denial.

The complexity of modern life is no servant to adversity at such times. And that adds to our inability to face sudden trauma.

When men were hunters and gatherers, life was probably more hazardous than it is today . . . but also far simpler.

True, a man could not sleep securely without wondering whether a grizzly or some crazed barbarian might attack in the middle of the night and steal away his woman or the next day's meal. But at the well-being level of existence, I contend, life back then was far more simple in the age of tribalism. A wife was probably pleased when she saw her husband on the horizon dragging their gutted dinner behind him. She celebrated his bravery, stealth, and courage, all of which made him a good provider and protector. Likewise, after being with smelly, unshaven men for days, his wife looked pretty good smiling at the door of their hut. The aroma of scrambled reptile eggs and a warm brew made life seem pretty good. As this man climbed under the skins at night, with his wife snuggled against him, he probably thought dimly to himself, *It just doesn't get any better than this!*

Today, life has become far more complex, and the chances of taking a hit come from a number of places. Some barbaric "sugar daddy" in a nice suit instead of a loin cloth might entice a younger man's wife away from him, and it may be corporate raiders who steal the evening meal. The daily reverses of fortune via the stock market, economic downturns—mixed with the unrealistic expectations for what we think life should give us—well . . . it's no wonder men are slowly cracking under the normal American way of doing things. But all the while, we're supposed to act as if we're handling everything well.

Yes, our pressure-cooker society brings us to emotional overload just *waiting* for adversity to drop a cement suitcase on the camel's breaking back. Some of you know what I mean because you've been hit with multiple stressors in a short amount of time. And you're probably wondering why you're having difficulty recovering. You're "supposed" to be able to handle it, right? Researchers Thomas

Holmes and Richard Rahe developed their now famous Holmes-Rahe Life Stress Scale which assigns various scores to different kinds of adversities. Heading their list are such things as: death of a spouse (100 points), followed by the crisis of divorce, separation, imprisonment, being fired, and loss of a close friend, etc. Their research showed that when scores reached 200 and beyond over the course of a year, the person became physically ill. Lower scores revealed that certain emotional and mental malfunctions were inevitable. This pioneer research shows that adversity has a profound impact upon the human psyche. It also demonstrated differing stressors produce differing emotional tolls upon men and women.

Dr. Michael Rutter, of the University of London, developed three categories for rating the stress-response to traumatic events. Rutter's classifications include: (1) Events resulting in the loss of a relationship; (2) events that cannot be controlled, therefore producing feelings of helplessness; (3) events that have long-lasting consequences. For men, something like divorce would be in the first category, while being in an accident or natural disaster the second. Chronic illness or suffering a physical disability would fit in the third classification. Of course, some life events overlap and expand into additional categories, but for the purposes of this chapter these categories will provide a helpful framework around which we can look at the differing types of adversity men face. Men especially have difficulty coping with adversity in all three of these categories.[1]

Loss of Relationships

When I lead men's conferences, I normally ask the men to comment about their relationships. I ask them who their best friend is. Inevitably, most say, "My wife." Sometimes

I see this as unfortunate. Why? Because for some men their wife is their *only* friend. At least, their response shows that when they think of relationships they think of marriage first.

Whether or not a married man has "buddies" to turn to, the primary relationship in his life is the one with his wife. Therefore, when a marriage breaks up due to divorce or death, men find themselves alone and at the mercy of some overwhelming reactions. It is sometimes assumed men do not suffer as greatly after a divorce as women do. But groundbreaking research by Wallerstein and Blakeslee has shown otherwise. They conclude,

> The idea that divorce can have long-lasting effects comes as a surprise to many people, including many mental health experts. Most Americans find comfort in the belief that time heals all wounds. The effects of divorce, it is said, last two or three years. . . . We have found that it takes women an average of three and one half years and men two and one half to reestablish a sense of external order after the separation.[2]

Because women are known more for their relational skills—and by comparison most men never measure up to the relational expectations of women—the impact of marital failure on men is sometimes ignored. The reality noted in the research is that younger men *some ten years after a divorce* are tragically depicted as "sad, bewildered, and unfocused." It is as if they are saying, "Look at me, I'm a failure."[3] In general, men who suffer divorce in their twenties have fewer social supports and friends than do women. They tend to be loners even if they don't think of themselves that way. They are uninvolved in clubs and community activities. Their only social network is usually work peers, other girlfriends, and their diminishing ties to

children, if any, and their former wives. Wallerstein summarizes the experience of one man who probably speaks for
many men, saying, "He feels unimportant, not needed, and
unloved."[4]

A few older men who have remarried happily (usually
to younger women) positively comment that divorce was
the greatest thing that could have happened to them. I wonder. Research in this area portrays another side. Men in
their forties and fifties can be extremely lonely, and instead
of finding comfort in their own inner resources (which
would include spiritual resources) or friends, they quickly
seek their needed comfort in female companionship. Half
of the older men in Wallerstein and Blakeslee's study are
seen as a picture of "intense isolation and deprivation."
They conclude, "Older women rebuild nests and networks
but continue to feel lonely, yet the plight of many older men
is worse. Uninterested in clubs, churches, political organ-
izations, and community associations, they have no life
outside work and even have trouble reaching out to their
children. A decade after divorce, a quarter of the older men
in our study remain isolated."[5]

One of the additional adverse effects divorce brings
upon men is when they lose the custody and involvement
with their children. I have come to think of this "effect" as
a man's *shadow grief.* This is a grief that a man carries
around, like a shadow following him into the depths of his
being, because he is no longer a key player, or a player at
all, in his children's lives. This has nothing to do with child
support or visiting rights. It has to do with the deep sadness
a man feels when there has been a severance in the ongoing
relationship with his kids.

Sometimes, the loss is more than just psychological or
geographical. The sense of loss, due to a spouse's death, is
crushing for men. For the man who loses his wife, the ad-

justment can be near impossible. He may *appear* to do well on the surface, but that's because we men have become masters at masking our true feelings. Unless someone really knows us well, our grief probably goes unnoticed. One researcher states boldly, "If there is a sex difference in conjugal bereavement reactions, it is *the man who suffers more* both physically and psychologically."[6] The writer goes on to point out that men generally view the death of their wives as "dismemberment," while women view the death of their husbands as "abandonment."

This insight confirms my own counseling experience. I think men are often surprised to learn that losing their wife feels more like losing a limb (or a part of themselves) than losing an important relationship with a loved one. The false appearance we men perpetuate—of being able to move on more quickly after a death—is explained by our inability or unwillingness to display grief openly. Studies, however, reveal that we have more guilt after the death of our wives. Women, on the other hand, demonstrate far more open displays of emotion.[7] Since women have more social supports in women friends who become grief partners, they usually fare better in the long term, and work toward a healthy acceptance of death. Men try to soothe the pain by marrying again as quickly as possible!

What About the Grief?

I was serving as Coordinating Chaplain for the Delta 191 crash at Dallas-Fort Worth Airport in August of 1985. In the midst of giving death notifications and doing grief work with families and survivors (136 people were killed), a well-dressed man appeared out of nowhere with tears in his eyes and asked if he could talk to me. We went off to the side of the DFW Hilton lobby. I asked him if he had lost someone on the flight. Through his tears his said, "Yes, my ex-wife." He went on to explain how he had been divorced from this woman for ten years. She had remarried and so had he. *So why is he here?* I wondered. He finally blurted out, "I wish I could have told her that being married to her wasn't as bad as I made her think it was . . . I really did love her." I told him to communicate his feelings to her new husband and her family. As quickly as he came, he left. But I thought to myself, *Remarried—but not recovered!*

Another illustration of how men deal with the loss of their primary relationship comes from a death-and-dying seminar I attended. When the presenter was talking about men who lose their spouses, he said briefly, "The statistics on remarriage rates by widowers argue that men are looking around at their wife's funeral for someone to take her place." He then added, "It's often their wife's best friend or some widowed old flame from high school who fills the terrifying emptiness."

My conclusion is that men, in spite of how they may appear, do not handle the grief of divorce or death well. These are critical times when men need the loving support and understanding of the church and some male friends who can help them face their grief. Seldom is it offered.

There is another loss that is even worse for some men.

Our children represent all that is innocent and hopeful in our lives. Therefore, when a child dies tragically in some kind of untimely accident or senseless act of violence, it sets off the worst kind of rage and shock in parents. No matter what the age of the child, both the mother and father have lost all their hopes, dreams, and ambitions for that child. They feel that they have not only lost a child but the child's future. Words like "assaulted, victimized, disabled, and mutilated" are often used to describe the experience.

Flight 191 took 136 lives. Among them was a twelve-year-old girl and her mother. When I met the father at the DFW Hilton, he wasn't saying anything. After taking him to my room and asking for photographs of his wife and daughter, he said, "She's my only child." He then slammed his fist through the coffee table in front of us. As I looked at the photo, association with my own life set in. I had a twelve-year-old daughter too. As I thought of what I'd be feeling if I had lost my precious Ashley, tears sprang to my eyes. As I handed the picture back, I pulled the young man toward my chest and we both began to cry. Tears flowed as he uttered, "She's my life." It struck me that even though he had lost both his wife and daughter, he felt more initial grief for his little girl. Such is the depth of grief men experience for their children.

Men deal with the loss of a child in a radically different way than their wives. This difference often creates an extreme disturbance of the marital relationship. Since, in Western culture, men have been conditioned to exert more emotional control than women, they often turn inside to deal with their loss. This lack of communication approach frustrates the wife, and she can't believe he doesn't say or vent anything. One man I know went back to work the day after his daughter was tragically killed. His wife couldn't believe it. She was completely immobilized in her grief and could not go outside the house. She was looking for his strength and compassion. But he could not stand being in the house where he had last seen his daughter. Men need time and distance to know how to approach pain. We need to circle it for a while. Going back to work for him was not denial of his feelings but, in fact, a very important first step in dealing with his grief.

Because men traditionally have seen themselves as the providers, protectors, and problem-solvers for the household, they in particular often feel they failed in not ade-

quately protecting their child from harm. One man felt he
had failed terribly by owning a home with a swimming pool
in which his five-year-old daughter drowned. Another man
was away on a business trip when his son was hit by a
drunk driver and killed. He felt had he been home, the tragedy might not have happened.

When men are confronted with the sudden death of
their own child,[8] they are characteristically "out of sync"
with their wives in dealing with the tragedy. They are often
unable to communicate about their feelings and have a tendency to blame themselves or someone else. One researcher observes, "Although partners may have pulled together to meet crises in the past, they will have to recognize
that they will seldom be in the same place at the same time
in their grief process and that this does not mean that they
do not still love one another."[9]

One final note: It is not unusual to see the couple's sexual relationship greatly affected by the loss. Since sexual
intimacy involves deep passions and feelings, either husband or wife may not want to open up this area for a while,
lest they tap into painful emotions. In addition, what may
be comforting for one partner during this time may be
something the other cannot endure. Some experts believe
it is not unusual for a couple's sexual relationship to be dis-
continued for as long as two years after the death of a child.

My conclusion based on the above examples and research is that men characteristically do not deal with the
loss of relationships well. If we were smart we would look
more closely at how women and men in other cultures deal
with loss issues. Mediterranean, African, Polynesian, and
Latin cultures allow men far more physical and emotional
expressions of grief during such difficult times. Personally,
I am envious of the cultural freedom they experience in this
regard.

But there is another aspect of adversity that causes men to discover their own unique reactions. Nothing disturbs a man more than feeling completely *out of control.* We will turn our attention to this next.

For Thought and Discussion

1. What relationship do you fear losing more than any other? Why is this so?
2. What kinds of relationship losses have you suffered? Do you think you have survived them well? What did you find most helpful during the initial stages (first week, first month)? How about during the next year?
3. Any new reflections on this loss, as a result of reading thus far?

Notes

1. Categories quoted in the book, *Winning Life's Toughest Battles*, by Dr. Julias Segal (New York: McGraw-Hill, 1986), p. 7.
2. Judith S. Wallerstein and Sandra Blakeslee, *Second Changes* (New York: Tichnor & Fields, 1989), pp. xi-xii.
3. Ibid., p. 222.
4. Ibid., p. 225.
5. Ibid., p. 45.
6. Research done by Stroebe & Stroebe, 1983, and quoted in the book, *Grief, Dying and Death*, Therese A. Rando (Champaign, Ill.: Research Press Co., 1984), p. 145.
7. Ibid., p. 145.
8. I am making a distinction here between sudden death and long-term illness leading to death because both women and men have a much longer time to process the event. Both kinds

are tragic, but the research suggests that sudden, unexpected deaths are far more difficult, especially when victimization or mutilation is involved.

9. Therese A. Rando, *Grief, Dying and Death*, p. 124.

Out of Control

Several weeks ago I was to fly from Philadelphia to Denver with a short layover in Chicago. When I arrived at my gate I found a seat and began reading my morning paper. I noticed the young girl next to me reading a book entitled *How to Edit*. I asked if she was an editor, and then small-talked my way into saying that I was on my way to meet with a publisher. She was impressed!

Throughout our conversation I noticed a business-suited man pacing back and forth in front of us. I hadn't noticed that our departure time had passed. After an hour delay, we were allowed to board, only to sit in the aircraft another hour waiting for fog to lift. Guess who ended up sitting next to me?

No, not the young editor . . . the pacing, now belted-in and even more disturbed businessman. He turned every which way, breathed heavily, rustled his paper, and finally pushed the light for the flight attendant. When she arrived, he laid a real power trip on her. He was one of those gold-club, ambassador-priority, red-carpet-class frequent flyers who somehow got stuck in econo-class next to me! And, of course, he had a *v-e-r-y* important meeting he had to get to in Los Angeles. She appeased him by letting him move to an aisle seat and giving him a free drink (at 9:00 A.M.).

Here was a man out of control and feeling utterly helpless, because with all his connections, clout and clubs, he couldn't do one thing about the fog. In short, he brought more adversity to an already adverse situation.

Now, I would hate to label this experience "traumatic," thus trivializing things like earthquakes, war, and major catastrophes. But to this poor man, it *was* traumatic. (By the way, when we finally landed in Chicago, we found out that all connecting fights had been canceled because of the fog!) I use this story to illustrate a fundamental phenomenon men experience at certain kinds of events. I too was frustrated and felt out of control, but in this instance I wasn't as obnoxious!

The kind of events that truly make men feel out of control are far more severe than being delayed at an airport. These events are some of the worst and unkindest of arrows which pierce our male armor.

Dr. Julius Segal, who worked with Vietnam POWs, writes,

> Try to imagine yourself as a captive. The activities you take for granted are no longer under your control. You cannot eat when you are hungry, enjoy a walk or a nap when you feel like it, or even urinate or defecate when nature calls. Your entire life has slipped out of your grasp.
>
> Most of the POWs I've talked with say that the realization they had lost command over their existence was the really awful thing about their ordeal. Losing control over their daily lives was more critical than

their more exotic and widely publicized sufferings—
the threats of execution, hunger, beatings, torture, and
isolation.[1]

You may recall the tragedy of the Navy F–14 Tomcat that
smashed headlong into a Nashville home, killing all the oc-
cupants and the two pilots. A neighbor across the street immediately rushed to the site where the home once stood. He
tried to help, but the fireball still engulfed the home. With
press cameras rolling, he detailed what he saw and how he
had tried to get near the crash to see if there were any survivors. His tearful eyes expressed the masculine dilemma
at times like these, "I felt so helpless. I couldn't do anything." Men, it seems, don't do well when they can do nothing! Women sometimes think we men are control freaks. We
always have to be in charge or in control of things. When
we can't, we either fall apart or blow up.

Sitting in your armchair, reading this book, you may ob-
ject. *Not me*. Really? Imagine yourself in the following situation. . . .

Into the Darkness

You are walking out of your local supermarket with your
six-months-pregnant wife. It's Friday evening, and you're
looking forward to going home, having a good meal, and
settling down to a movie on the VCR. You're a young businessman in your first job out of college. You've been married two years, and now your firstborn is just a few months
from making you the proudest of fathers. As you walk
toward the parking lot, you put the two bags of groceries in
one hand, reach down with your free hand, and take your
wife's arm. As she looks up at you, you notice how radiant
she looks in the early evening sunlight.

As you open the car door for her, you feel a blow to the back of your head. You are momentarily unconscious. When you awake, you find yourself in the darkness of the car's trunk. Above the road noise, you occasionally hear the voice of your wife and another man. You hear normal talking, then crying, then screaming. You think about kicking the trunk open and trying to escape, but then the car could speed off with your wife and unborn child. But if you do nothing, you don't know what might happen inside the car. Your soul is tortured with rage, fear, and uncertainty. You don't know what to do, and finally you decide you can do nothing but wait.

After hours of driving, hearing your wife plead for the life of her unborn child, the car stops. The trunk opens and there is a ski-masked man pointing a gun directly at your head. He tells you to get out, which you do. You see your wife in the car looking back at you nervously. The gunman then tells her to get out and pushes both of you to a nearby ATM machine. He tells you to withdraw all the money in your account, which you do. Taking the money, he jumps into the car and speeds off.

You turn and embrace your wife, thanking God that she has been spared. But now the reality of all that happened is revealed. The sexual molestation and the threats of being killed.

How did you feel, standing so briefly in the shoes of the husband in this real-life story? His self-esteem was crushed by the experience, and his trust for people completely eroded. The depression and feelings of incompetence eventually cost him his job. He would have panic attacks at making even the slightest of decisions. In short, he never could regain a sense of control over his life or the event. His wife never wanted to be touched again sexually, and the man became so depressed he had to be hospitalized. Now, he survives on anti-depressants.

I wonder at this point whether my male readers can identify with this young man. He found himself in a situation where he could do nothing to protect his wife and unborn child from the harm. I'm not sure any of us would have felt differently.

I think that in our Christian circles the issue of control has been given a bad rap lately. *Control* is a "bad" word these days, often given a negative, almost "unbiblical" spin. But are there positive aspects of control, too? After all, aren't we to be controlled by the Holy Spirit of God? Self-controlled? Are men control freaks—or does a certain amount of control play a very important role in good mental health?

Researchers confirm that crime victims (both male and female) see themselves as weak, helpless, needy, frightened, and out of control.[2] As a result, those who are victimized see their views of the world and themselves seriously challenged, if not destroyed. It is as if one's entire assumptions about life are shattered, leaving the individual with no functional meaning or resources for coping. "If bad things can happen to me, then they can happen again, and again, and again," so the victim thinks. The emotional/mental logic is inescapable. Even among dedicated Christians I have seen the emotional logic throw out their belief in a loving, benevolent God who should have prevented such an event. Even their Christian worldview is seriously challenged by the painful realities of catastrophic evil.

Some would suggest it is a good thing when men finally lose control of something, or completely give up control of their lives. But I would differ with the viewpoint. I once asked a friend of mine who is a psychologist if he could reduce mental illness down to its most simple essence.

Without thinking much thought, he blurted out, "Control issues. The mentally ill either try to overcontrol their lives, or have it completely out of control. The imbalance is what leads to severe mental disturbances."

Later, I learned his off-the-cuff assessment was acutely on target. On the subject of psychological control, one specialist concludes,

> Excessive controls interrupt the process (of adjusting to traumatic events), change the state of the person to some form of denial and may prevent complete processing of the event. Failures of control lead to excessive levels of emotion, flooding, and retraumatization, causing entry into intrusive states. Optimal controls slow down recognition processes and so provide tolerable doses of new information and emotional responses.[3]

Our task, men, is to learn the balance between what we *can* and should control . . . and what we cannot.

My impatient friend on the plane was trying to overcontrol an impossible situation. And he was feeling angry and justified in spraying anger on others. This guy needed to learn patience.

But the man who feels he has lost control of his life due to a traumatic event needs to *regain* a sense of control, or at least a certain healthy measure of it. I will talk about this process in a later chapter.

The essence of what I'm saying is this: When men face something in which we lose complete control, we feel helpless and weak. This is normal for men to feel in traumatic situations. It demonstrates we are very much alive and human.

I believe we need to affirm this aspect of men in adversity and help them to regain a new sense of control. We are not sick "weaklings" for having balanced and healthy feelings of helplessness. We are simply reacting humanly and normally to abnormal situations.

On the other hand, we cannot let our *initial* reactions lead us down to utter despair. Depression and a host of other problems result when a man concludes that life itself is cruel toward him, and no matter what he does he is powerless to change anything. Warren Farrell puts in this category the black male and the Native American.

> Indian men could not adequately protect their food, water, and land from white invaders. Despite legends and myths that trained the Indian man to sacrifice himself, when legends, bows, and arrows could not keep up with technology, guns, and bullets, his family was confined to the reservations of their defeat. Unable to protect by killing buffalo or by making a killing on Wall Street, the Indian man became disposable. He received little love, and with little love, found much liquor.
>
> Similarly, as those black men with a slave heritage entered an industrialized era without adequate training to protect their families, they were also rejected by women. Only the black male performers—usually physical performers such as Wilt Chamberlain and Magic Johnson—found thousands of women. Black men who could not perform were subject to ridicule in novels and films (e.g., *The Color Purple, The Women of Brewster Place*).
>
> As a result of this inadequate preparation to protect, many African-American men often chose aberrant, quick fix, lottery-type attempts to make it—via drug dealing, gambling, or the lottery itself. When these methods failed to bring them the money to protect, they, as with Indian men, found themselves inadequate for women's love, gambling for a last hope of love, and, if they failed, drugging themselves to death.[4]

I contend the experience of African-American and Indian-American males, though greater in numbers, is not all that different in kind than our upper-middle-class white suburban males. The exception may be that we Anglos have learned to conceal our failure, pain, and despair better. Our "alcoholism" does not necessarily put us on the streets, but it is more socially accepted—via country clubs, cocktail parties, and even church and community involvement.

Unemployment

Jack was numbed by the news. After ten years he was being indefinitely laid off from his job. Oh, sure, the rumors about layoffs were always circulating around the plant, but he had reasoned since he was a foreman with ten years experience, any layoffs would start at the bottom. What was worse than thinking about the layoff was how he was going to break the news to his wife. She was planning on putting an addition on the house and renovating their out-of-date kitchen. How could he explain to his kids that he had no job, no immediate hope of getting one, and no knowledge as to whether he would be called back to his old job?

With increasing frequency, Jack's experience is becoming commonplace. When unemployment strikes, it surfaces a man's worst fears about his ability to provide for his family. In the face of joblessness, he must also face himself as a failure. Researchers have found that sudden, unexpected unemployment has devastating effects on the primary breadwinner (usually male). In communities where large-scale layoffs have taken place, mental hospital admissions, suicides, homicides, and cardiovascular disease all increase proportionally. Other effects observed are lowered self-esteem, anxiety, depression, and a disruption of normal family functioning.[5]

Regardless of the social transformation of roles among men during the past several decades, the reality is that men still feel responsible for providing for their families. Men also find a significant amount of their self-identity in work, therefore, the loss of employment represents not only the loss of the money, but the loss of their *value* as an individual as well. Work is also the significant integrator of a man's life. It structures his day and determines the amount of time spent with family and other activities. Because his life and schedule is disrupted, all the family routines are affected. This can easily lead to increased tension at home as his wife and children become resentful of the disruption. The longer a man remains jobless, the more he begins to feel hopeless and out of control. One man I know became so down on himself—though his credentials and work experience were unbelievable—he began to think he would never work again. I laughed when he told me, and then I quickly realized this was no laughing matter. His self-esteem had dropped so low, he really believed it. Even though the adversity of unemployment is listed here, it could be included in the next section. For some men, long periods of unemployment or numerous layoffs have profound long-term effects on their lives and self-esteem.

Events With Long-Term Consequences

The bifocaled doctor looks across his desk, gazing alternately at you and the test results. Finally, he declares, "It doesn't look good. It's a metastatic tumor."

You say, "There must be a mistake. This couldn't happen to me." Why is this response so common?

I believe God has placed a mechanism within our hearts, commonly and mistakenly called *denial*, that im-

mediately kicks in and protects us from the too-sudden reality of things like a shortened life-span. This kind of denial
serves a very healthy purpose. It buys us some adjustment
time. I believe being made in the image of God means we
are created for eternity. We have immortal souls created for
far more than our earthly lives. Because of our fallen nature, we are bound to the earthly, mortal processes and diseases. Therefore, an announcement that the death process
is upon us more swiftly than expected is not only "impossible," it's an intrusion into our normal psyche.

Consequently, we deny disability, sickness, and death.
We rationalize it and fight against it in an attempt to beat
the odds. In this arena, too, it seems we do not do well facing adversity. Whether a man has to live with cancer or
AIDS, or is confined to a wheelchair, we find it difficult to
grasp the reality of such hardships.

The biggest adjustment a man must make is to accurately assess what he can and cannot do in his new condition. This first, natural thing we do, of course, is to assess
our chances at "getting back to normal." Unfortunately, we
may be required to adjust to a "new normal"—not the old
normal we once enjoyed. For instance, an accountant confined to a wheelchair may still be able to practice his pro-
fession, but have a hard time in his sexual relationship with
his wife. What is sexually possible and enjoyable is likely
to pose a tougher problem for him than his limited mobility
at work. For an artist losing the use of a drawing hand may
have more far-reaching consequences than for other disabled men. Several studies have revealed that non-sympto-
matic HIV-positive males are more highly stressed than
those with visible symptoms. They feel like "walking time
bombs, knowing they are not completely healthy, yet not
having any serious signs of illness."[6] (Since the AIDS crisis
has affected far more men than women, this means that of

the estimated two million asymptomatic HIV-positives, the larger percentage is men.) So these men are having to carry the invisible burden of this sentence of death upon them— while generally being ignored or scorned by the church— and unable to know what disability and suffering lie ahead.

When men are faced with adverse circumstances that have long-term consequences, they also face some unique conflicts. One man who was shot and robbed at gunpoint often awoke to dreams of reversing the situation, whereby he held the gun on his attacker. (Women, on the other hand, develop themes of self-recrimination and the inability to fight off their attackers. One woman, who had been raped and asked why she didn't fight against it, said, "How could I have gorged out his eyes? I never could have forgiven myself.") And the long-term effects may change from psychological distress to outward and physical distress. Many men won't acknowledge emotional injuries as legitimate and feel unjustified in seeking sympathy or help.[7] This has often been the case with war veterans. Those with no visible physical injuries feel they have nothing to complain about, so they bury their feelings of guilt, shame, and anger. The long-term effects are seen in abusive relationships and the inability to hold jobs, while reliving the nightmares of fire-fights, officer "fraggings," and the killing of women and children. One vet who had warned his good friend to not go near a crying baby lying in a village road watched in horror as his friend was "blown to bits" along with the child who was booby-trapped. This same vet found it increasingly difficult to pick up his baby daughter when she cried, some ten years after Nam.[8] His wounds suffered in the rice paddies of Vietnam are not visible but, nevertheless, very real, and alive and well. Adversity creates a pain that stays . . . and *spreads.*

I had just finished speaking at a men's conference when

a man immediately cornered me. "I was an alcoholic, and my wife finally divorced me," he said. "Over time, I saw less and less of my kids. Now they're all grown and they want nothing to do with me. Last year I came to know Christ as my Savior, and now I want to right my wrongs and try to reestablish a relationship with my children. What can I do?"

My heart went out to this dear brother, and I suggested he start with his grandchildren and work back up the relational ladder. Grandchildren don't have the same emotional history, and they are probably far more forgiving. Here was a man still grieving the loss of his children some twenty years after a divorce. He was brokenhearted that there seemed so little he could do to remedy the situation.

As he walked away, I too felt his sadness for a situation beyond his control. But I believed that he *could* make some steps toward rebuilding and find his way to a "new normal," though life would not be as it was before alcoholism and divorce and estrangement. If he would open himself to new possibilities, and make even the first attempts at letting go of regrets, he could begin something new.

What the last two chapters have affirmed is that men, by almost any statistic, do not handle adversity well. With all the emphasis during the last decades on women's rights and women's issues, perhaps it is time to also address the shocking data about men. Without being alarmist or sexist, I do agree with Warren Farrell in his somewhat humorous but serious call for the government to establish an Office of Men's Health. He suggests,

> An Office of Men's Health could educate men about why men are seven times more likely than women to be arrested for drunk driving while only three times more likely than women to be hospitalized for alcoholism.

We often interpret women's increased drinking and smoking as reflections of women's increased stress level (which it often is) but rarely interpret the facts that men are three times more likely to be alcoholics and more likely to die of lung cancer as reflections of men's continuing higher stress level. In brief, we keep ourselves open to new ways of understanding (and helping) women, which is wonderful, but fail to use the same mind-set to better understand (and help) men.

We have a choice. We can continue socializing our sons to fight our fires and be amazed when they fight their feelings: . . . to develop programs to prevent men from being 95% of the prisoners and 85% of the homeless; to do for men what we would be doing for women if women used to live one year less but now live seven years less, used to be equal victims of the fifteen causes of death and were suddenly the first victims of every one of the fifteen major causes of death.[9]

In the next chapter I will try to provide some insight into how we as men may be able to stem the tide of this male malaise as we take new strides to help each other—and ourselves—handle adversity.

For Thought and Discussion

1. Would you describe yourself as a "control freak"? Would your friends or spouse agree with you?
2. Can you identify some of your control strategies that help you regain control when you feel "out of control"?
3. Do you feel being "out of control" is ever healthy? Have you ever "overcontrolled" a situation, creating an even greater adversity for yourself?

Notes

1. Julias Segal, *Winning Life's Toughest Battles*, p. 38.
2. Charles E. Figley, ed., *Trauma and Its Wake* (New York: Brunner/Mazel Psychological Stress Series, 1985), p. 22.
3. Ibid., p. 56.
4. Warren Farrell, *The Myth of Male Power* (New York: Simon & Shuster, 1993), p. 207.
5. Patricia Voydanoff, "Unemployment: Family Strategies for Adaptation," in *Stress and the Family, Vol. II: Coping With Catastrophe*, Charles Figley and Hamilton McCubbin, eds. (New York: Brunner/Mazel, 1983), p. 91.
6. Quoted in *No Longer Immune*, Craig Kain, editor, American Association of Counseling and Development (Alexandria, Va., 1989), p. 63.
7. Morton Bard & Dawn Sangrey, *The Crime Victim's Book*, 2nd edition (New York: Brunner/Mazel, 1986), pp. 76–85.
8. Charles R. Figley, editor, *Stress Disorders Among Vietnam Veterans* (New York: Brunner/Mazel, 1978), p. 263.
9. Warren Farrell, *The Myth of Male Power*, pp. 197–198.

Unhealthy Ways Men Deal With Adversity

The genetic code I inherited from my parents is Irish/ English in origin. Years ago I visited my ancestral roots in the month of May. I expected it to be quite pleasant. I was raised in Kansas on the great plains, where I've seen drifts of snow higher than my bedroom window. I've been to North Dakota in the winter, and the Ukraine in December. But I have never been so cold in my life as I was that May in England. The bone-chilling Arctic drafts coming off the North Sea and the English Channel cut through the several layers of clothing I wore. I gained a new appreciation for English wool, and a compassion for American "New" Englanders who are sometimes accused of being emotionally cold. If they're cold, it's because they're cold!

When it comes to the way we men relate to each other, to life, and to the way we handle troubles, I think there is something to be said about this climatic explanation of human behavior. Many have observed that men whose forefathers come from the Northern European strain of mas-

culinity have received a very "cold and aloof" way of
approaching life. Yes, there are exceptions. But what this
means in terms of handling adversity is that Northern European men, for the most part, have developed a certain
"stiff upper lip" (Brits), or the Germanic "dispassionate or-
dered life," or the Slavic "gut it out" approach to life. The
common denominator for men is that feelings are unimportant, irrelevant, and in the final analysis, a threat to male
survival.

On the other hand, the warmer the climate, the more in-
tune and expressive men are with their emotions. Look at
the Italians, Spanish, Mediterranean, Polynesian, and Latin
cultures. In these cultures, men openly weep, embrace,
hold hands, and outwardly enjoy life with an emotional
gusto not often seen in Western males.

Whatever the real roots, many of us come from homes
or traditions that have taught us approaches to life and its
hard times that are not healthy or helpful. Too many of us
spend a large amount of time and energy doing things that
may, in fact, be counterproductive to the healthy adjust-
ments we need to make when trouble hits.

Every human being has a certain set of learned behavior
pattern mechanisms that actually work . . : in a way . . . for
a while. Many of us rationalize, withdraw, blame, or deny
our mess. We keep people at a safe distance and keep the
problem emotionally at bay, and think that our effort is
"working." In some sense, these dodges let us off the hook.
When adversity strikes, it is only natural to fall back on the
coping strategies that have worked for us in other problem-
solving situations. We naively assume that what worked for
lesser problems will work for more traumatic ones. There
is some truth to this assumption, which is what makes it
deadly.[1]

Unfortunately, we all have a tendency to stick with a

coping strategy long after it ceases to work. We're like a guy who keeps popping pain-killers to deaden the pain of a bad headache—thinking it will cure his headache—when really his neck is cracked. Pain-killers work . . . for a normal, garden-variety headache.

On a more serious note, whatever coping techniques men are using in our society, most counselors will tell you "they're not working." Ellis Cose raises a disturbing question: "If women feel more pain, why are men self-destructing?"[2] From his in-depth interviews of men from all walks of life, he concluded, "We don't have a happy bunch of men . . . they look good on the outside, but they are not happy on the inside."[3] He goes on to detail the stories of men suffering in secret, while very concerned about the social disapproval of appearing to be in need. Men, simply put, think they are not supposed to feel pain, talk about their pain, or complain about life. Therefore, they just "grit their teeth," "bite the bullet," and "bear the pain . . . like a man." Another researcher suggests "we have created a society in which men are so fearful of not measuring up that many would rather succeed at suicide than be perceived as failures."[4]

These observations make it imperative to have a proper understanding of what unhealthy coping mechanisms look like. Therefore, what I would like to do in this chapter is to reveal ways in which men attempt to deal with adversity which are not productive. In the long run, they may even become self-destructive.

Silence Is Not Always Golden

Shakespeare seems to have understood the human heart better than many modern mental health professionals. On the subject of dealing with loss and adversity, the English

bard says, "Give sorrow words: the grief that does not speak
. . . whispers in the o'er-fraught heart and bids it break."[5]
The heart that does not speak of its pain breaks! This insight surfaces and, as well, critiques the male tendency to
use silence and denial as means of coping with the negative
and traumatic situations in our lives.

I must be honest at this point and admit to my own difficulty in breaking free from this misconception. Like most
men, I have serious difficulty in both naming and explaining my feelings when I get hit with a hard situation—especially to my wife. Feelings seem like some amorphous
floating fogs. Sure I can counsel other guys—but when it
hits me, it defies labels or words. Women find it so easy to
connect feelings with words, but for men, we by and large
do not have either the vocabulary or competency to adequately express our inner pain.

You need not feel incompetent about this. There may
well be a biological reason why it is so. Women's emotional
responses reside in both hemispheres of their brains.
Whereas in men, our emotional functions are concentrated
in the right hemisphere (making us half-wits emotionally—
I couldn't resist the joke!). Since verbal dexterity functions
are located on the left side in both brains, this creates critical differences between men and women. What connects
the two sides of the brain in both sexes is the *corpus cal-
losum*. In women, these connectors are thicker and more
bulbous, thus having greater efficiency in transmitting
thoughts or feelings from one side of the brain to the other.

Geneticist Anne Moir explains, "This means that more
information is being exchanged between the left and right
sides of the female brain . . . the more connections people
have . . . the more articulate and fluent they are. This finding provides a further explanation for women's verbal dexterity."[6]

This understanding of the male brain is good news for explaining why we can act like emotional "half-wits." But the explanation does not help our dilemma. Because we are at a disadvantage at putting feelings into words does not mean we should give up and remain mute. We *need* to speak and we need to name what's bothering us deep inside. We need to do something with our turmoil besides burying it within ourselves, or masking it with alcohol or work.

Now, some of us have tried to express our feelings of confusion. But we have not met with overwhelming success. Some of us have gotten the message, "Real men keep their problems to themselves." Or, "You're a man, you can figure it out on your own." It's compounded when you have a hard time finding the words to begin with.

When I have tried to put my deepest feelings into words for my wife, there are times she doesn't grasp my difficulty. What she thinks is the beginning of a long, juicy, emotionally laden conversation is in reality the end! She can ask, "How do you feel about this?" My silence for the next ten minutes drives her up the walls. Finally, after I have turned the question over and over in my mind, and attempted my best shot at trying to access my right emotional hemisphere, I walk back into the kitchen and say, "Bad." She looks at me strangely, having already moved on to more productive conversations with the pots and pans, and returns, "Bad. Is that it?"

"Yes, I feel bad." With that look of utter feminine amazement on her face, she answers, "After all this time, that's all you could come up with?"

So I am driven back into my cave of noncommunicating silence. I thought I was really making progress in this feeling stuff by even coming up with the articulation "bad."

Some men—thinking other men will better understand

a man's turmoil—have been "burned" when they've opened up and shared. I was once in one of those "accountable relationships" with another man. We met over lunch periodically to see how each other was doing. Usually, in the course of our time together, we got around to talking about things we were struggling with. Often the subject turned to marriage and family issues. He would ask, "How's Cinny doing?" Or, "Is your son doing any better?" Since this was an accountability thing, I took the bait, opened up, and told him. I shared the bad with the good, tried to be as honest as I could, and thought we were getting pretty close as brothers in the Lord.

Later, some of my personal disclosures were used against me in an attempt to disqualify me from ministry. His ego got in the way and he became an *emotional betrayer*. Some men are like this, and they are not "safe" to be around.

As men we need to fully realize what our rejection or abuse of another guy's trouble and emotions does to that man. Likewise, just because I have been burned by a few brothers, I can't let the experience drive me back into my self-contained and self-absorbed silence—even though it's tempting! Fortunately, over the years I've had one or two friends whom I could trust with my greatest trials and hurts. Without them, I don't know where I might be today. Probably still mumbling the word "bad."

As men we need to have someone in our life who understands and is not thrown by our difficulties. Who can see through our silent denial. Who can bear with us in our slowness in identifying feelings. Rejection or misunderstanding by other men, or their show of "superiority," just drives us deeper into despair and denial.

In the movie *The Doctor*, William Hurt plays a "very all-together," successful doctor. His life is the perfect American dream . . . until a malignant cancer is discovered in his throat. The movie realistically portrays a man desperately trying to verbalize his feelings of pain. His fellow doctors are of no help, and for whatever reasons, he doesn't let his own wife into his inner pain. He concludes no one can adequately understand what he is going through. His own medical expertise is more a curse than a help. In the midst of his confusion and anger, he forms a relationship with a fellow radiation-therapy patient. This fellow sufferer is the one who introduces and mentors the doctor into the world of shared pain and coping—a world he never knew as a physician.

This is what men need—someone who will walk with us in our lostness and sorrow. But before we can give words to our sorrow, we must be convinced that our silence is nothing more than a quiet conspiracy against our own mental health.

As I noted earlier—denial buys us some time to adjust to the adversity. But over time it only keeps our feelings from surfacing. When I speak of denial in men, sometimes there is a misunderstanding about the concept. The kind of mental functioning I'm talking about is not the kind that says, "My arm is not broken"—when in fact a bone is sticking out of the skin. This is not psychological denial but severe mental illness (as well as a broken bone). The kind of denial men use is when we know something is wrong within us. We feel the pain in our gut, but we don't reveal it to anyone. We may then try to deaden it with alcohol, drugs, sex, hobbies, work, or other escapes—just so we can remain in control and keep functioning. This exercise in denial makes us toxic carriers of an inward disease, while on the outside appearing as if we can handle anything. This is what produces the stats on men and self-destruction.

A primary means of deadening pain in men is through

the use and abuse of alcohol and drugs. Initially, when some severe adversity strikes, there may be a real need to take a tranquilizer or antidepressant in order to get through the normal functions of the day. But when drugs and alcohol become the primary or only means of coping, then there is an obvious problem. One disaster management specialist I know once told me somewhat jokingly, "After as many disasters as I have worked on, where I have to see so many human parts lying around, I don't go anywhere without my chaplain, my psychiatrist, and a bottle of Scotch—and not necessarily in that order." Even though the comment was in jest, I walked away wondering if the Scotch was his primary coping mechanism and maybe even this expert in the trauma field needed to unmask the dark terrors in his soul.

The Bind That Ties

The reality we face in regard to denial is a threefold bind.

First, I don't think women can or necessarily want to hear all the gory details of our pain. Underneath all of the rhetoric about the sensitive, *more-in-touch-with-his-feelings* kind of man that the '80s perpetuated is the reality that women deep down felt he was a wimp.[7] That's why *Time* magazine in 1990 declared the "Sensitive Male" gone, and the Pucci male models went from six feet tall to six feet two inches with expanded forty-two-inch chests. When a man shares too much inner pain with his wife, or woman-friend, I believe she begins to distrust his ability to protect and provide for her. The more he gets in touch with his feelings of failure, the more she concludes he cannot take care of her. In other words, women *say* they want to understand our pain, but they really can't handle the impact of it because it makes them feel insecure about their life with us.[8]

This can create quite a bind in a marriage. We need to be able to share our adversity with our wives, but don't be surprised when rejection or lack of understanding is the result.

The same difficulty exists in relation to other men. I believe men today long for deeper and more honest relationships with other men. My unsophisticated guess here is that this is what is really driving the three simultaneous men's movements. (Men going into the woods with other men to beat drums, Promise Keeper rallies in football stadiums, and the well-financed gay movement.) But herein lies a second bind. If we share our deepest feelings with some brother, we run the risk of being betrayed, or worse, being viewed as a failure because we can't "cut it" as a man. The "real men don't cry" attitude is still deeply embedded in our male culture. The old saying that "men don't bleed in public" is still written on our hearts. In corporate culture it is axiomatic. In the military, it is law.

So that leaves us with the third bind. This one is within ourselves. The conflict lies between living with hypocrisy (by not revealing what's really going on on the inside) and risking vulnerability. Adversity is bad enough by itself in making a man feel vulnerable and out of control. To take the gigantic risk of sharing how I feel with another human being makes a man feel even more vulnerable. Hence, the bind between honesty and vulnerability.

Even King David's court musician, Asaph, struggled with this bind. He wrote, "If I said, 'I will speak thus' [about my painful feelings], I would have betrayed this generation of your children. When I tried to understand all this, it was oppressive to me" (Psalm 73:15–16). He faced the same conflict between being honest about his feelings over

against what revealing his feelings would do to a generation
who thought his life was more spiritual!

Blaming and Shaming

A second way we can short-circuit healthy coping is
through the use of blame.

Blame and *shame* are the unhealthy brothers of denial.
Again, the compulsion to blame is the natural and normal
response to adverse events. Take any kind of traumatic situation and ask, "Are people coming out of the woodwork
claiming responsibility in the matter?" Only terrorists do
that, and we all know they're crazy!

When I worked as a counselor after the Delta crash, the
immediate response from family members and survivors
was to blame someone for what had happened. I had to realize this response was normal human functioning for
where they were at the time. Blame was attached to anyone
who might in any way have been responsible. First, it was
some kind of pilot error, then it got transferred to the air-
traffic controllers for not closing the airport during the
thunderstorm. The meteorologists were blamed for not
picking up the wind shear which was the cause of the
crash. Then the lack of Doppler radar at DFW was blamed,
and why the airport authorities hadn't purchased the latest
technology. Naturally, Delta Airlines was blamed, God was
blamed, and I even got my share of blame as God's repre-
sentative. The need to find and place blame is foundational
to the traumatic experience, but it is not a healthy coping
mechanism over time.

What blame does for us is reinforce our cognitive—or
reasoned—worldview while our emotional world is falling
apart. In other words, blame gives us the immediate rationale we need in order to keep functioning. It provides a tem-

porary meaning for the adversity.

Blaming keeps at bay that other nasty sense—that some defect in us caused the problem. This sense of personal defectiveness is known as *shame*. The father blames himself for building the swimming pool in which his child drowned. The fired employee blames himself for being useless, even though a hundred others got "downsized," too. A husband blames himself for not getting his wife to the "right" doctor when she dies of cancer. All these self-blaming responses reinforce our belief in a rational, cause-effect world. They also give us men a certain amount of illusionary control over the situation. At least by having someone to blame—even myself—it provides me with a sense of control over a situation which is virtually uncontrollable. In the short term it works, but over time, shame is poison to the soul.

Masking

In Elie Weisel's excellent play *The Trial of God*, the plot is built around a troupe of Purim players who arrive at a Russian tavern just after a pogrom against the Jewish population. The only Jews left in the little town are the tavern owner and his mentally disturbed daughter. When the players wish to put on a Purim play for the guests, the owner mocks at the celebration, saying instead they should put God on trial for allowing the execution of His people. The idea finds favor with the gathered group. A judge is appointed, a jury selected, and witnesses are named. Everyone puts on a mask representing their part. But who will be God's attorney?

An obscure, shadowy figure in the corner of the pub is enlisted to be God's counsel. As the trial proceeds, the shadowy counsel turns out to be brilliant. He defends God

with such logic and passion, many think the man must be a rabbi or at least a *Hasid*, a "righteous one." No one can counter his arguments in defending God's affairs in the world. At the end of the play/trial everyone takes off their masks. A hush of horror sets over everyone as God's attorney reveals who he really is . . . Satan![9]

The play illustrates how men can mask the dark, shadowy side of their pain and evil, while defending God with brilliance and passion. As men we learn early in life to wear the appropriate masks for the situation. We have our work mask, our church mask, our family mask, and our community masks. Therefore, when adversity hits us with its full impact, it is very easy to fall back on our well-honed masking abilities.

What is worse, sometimes our Christianity is nothing more than a mask we wear. Yes, there are men with deep, true, spiritual faith. But too many of us merely say the right Christian things like, "I know God is in control." Or, "All things work together for good." Or, "In everything give thanks." But underneath lies a cesspool of darkness, anger, and pain. We can mask our pain with almost anything—even God-talk.

We can also mask pain by becoming very protective of ourselves or others. I don't like being hurt. I don't like suffering loss, therefore it is easy to say, "I will never allow myself to be hurt again." I mask my pain by pulling in and not giving myself to anyone or anything. One "downsized" executive told me, "I will never trust another public company." Men who were burned in one marriage may say, "I'll never give my heart to another woman." Some men become overprotective so as to mask their own real failure.

Veterans trying to cope with the realities of war attempt to overprotect their wives and children. Having been harmed themselves, they do not want to see their loved ones harmed, so they go to extremes to keep them safe. One marine would not allow his wife to go out at night without him. A woman told me of her World War II dad, who so scrutinized all her boyfriends and drilled them about the details of their whereabouts, she finally left home at age seventeen—only to marry a Vietnam vet who repeated the pattern.

What masking is really about is avoidance. After the death of his only son, John immediately went back to work. He found all kinds of reasons to work extra hours and do special projects. In the eyes of his employer, John was "coping very well" with the death. In fact, his workaholic schedule was being driven by the masked pain of not wanting to be near his son's room. Every time his wife asked him what they should do with John Jr.'s belongings, he would just say, "I can't deal with that right now." Six months later, at the urging of a friend, he and his wife finally went into his son's room and cried their way through each article of clothing and memorabilia. At this point, his mask was taken off, and he began to face the dark reality of the loss of his son.

Crosby and Jose have noted,

> By keeping busy we defend ourselves against the anxiety that arises when we are doing nothing . . . keeping busy enables us to put our mental-emotional energy into the task at hand, thus diverting thoughts and feelings away from the death. As we struggle with our grief, we likely will have tasks to perform and worthwhile work to do. Keeping busy is, in itself, not wrong; the wrongness is in the fact that it turns into a dysfunctional strategy when it becomes the primary method of coping.[10]

The mask of avoidance can also be seen in taking trips,

spending lots of money (especially when large insurance checks show up), becoming uncharacteristically promiscuous, or making shrines of a departed loved-one's room. Each of these may work for a while, but they do not promote healthy healing.

Inflexibility

I am of the persuasion that men have incredible strengths. But as in so many other areas of life, our greatest asset can easily become our greatest liability. Generally speaking, men over the centuries have been capable of overthrowing tremendous odds simply by their sheer determination and discipline. They were remarkably goal-oriented, they endured pain, and denied themselves many pleasures in order to forge out the wilderness, build empires, or woo the woman they loved. Simply stated, nothing could deter them from their course. Tenacity is a great virtue.

When adversity wounds a man's spirit, though, it is so easy for tenacity to become *inflexibility*. We sort of retreat to hold our ground until the storm blows through. Here, we might learn the lesson of the palm tree which bends with the hurricane winds and rarely gets uprooted. Firmly entrenched oaks become quickly uprooted simply because their nature is to be unbending.

I have known many men who are more like inflexible oaks than palm trees. We also have our Christian version of oak trees. Some men think that to change course, or flex a little bit in the face of adversity, is to "compromise one's convictions," or "deny the truth." We can see this behavior demonstrated in the life of Job. He had as much stuff thrown at him as a man could possibly face at one time. He lost his children, his wealth, his reputation and standing in the community, and finally his health. The only thing God didn't allow Satan to take was his life . . . and of course, his very unsupportive wife.

Job rightfully argues his own righteous case before his friends and won't budge on his desire and demand that God answer him. Even though Job's friends are poor comforters bringing only blame and shame, Job holds to his convictions . . . until God speaks. After God speaks, Job is silent. This change in perspective, which the Bible calls *repentance* (toward God and his friends), marks the upward conclusion of the story. (See Job 42:1–16.) Job never had his question answered as to why he suffered, but God had to bring him to the point where he was willing to give up his old way of thinking. His way of thinking was centered around his assumptions and convictions about *how* God should work. In one sense, God had to shatter Job's wrong assumptions in order to bring about the change in his soul. Is there a truth in this for us—something about the way God works that we are afraid to face?

What Job says to me is that when adversity strikes, we men need to loosen up a little. We need to see beyond the adversity to what God might be doing to change something within us. When we face adversity, it is only proper and good to affirm our convictions, or stand fast on the basis of the truths we believe. But eventually we have to face firm reality. God did not answer Job's fundamental question, so he had to change. Likewise, we may need to make some necessary changes in order to survive or heal well. Individuals who are rigid and inflexible have a more difficult time making the kinds of changes they need to make in order to facilitate proper adjustment. Studies have shown how Holocaust survivors were the ones who learned to adapt quickly, thereby bringing about some order to their lives—while the aged and inflexible just lay down and died!

Refusing Help

I really hate asking for directions. I don't know if I think it is just plain wimpish, or that it takes all the challenge out of life, or I'm just lazy. But I know it drives my wife crazy. Her first instinct is to stop and ask someone.

I think this masculine behavior trait unfortunately spills over into how we attempt to handle adversity. Men basically go it alone and find it very difficult to ask for help. I must say I am a little perplexed by this trait, because I see men ask for help in so many other areas. Plumbing can break, and we are quick on the phone to call a friend or a plumber. Male executives spend thousands on consultants to come in and help them in areas where they need expertise. Young professional athletes can say to an older one, "Show me how to throw that pitch." In these areas, it seems very natural and common.

Why then do we struggle with asking for some kind of emotional or relational help? Bestselling author Deborah Tannen has noted that whereas women relate to the world as a *community of relationships* waiting to be discovered, men relate to the world on the basis of a *hierarchical social order*.[11] In other words, men have difficulty asking for help because they do not want to be placed in an inferior position. To be in a therapist's office or to say to a friend that we are not doing well is to risk being in this inferior position. It's a one-upmanship game we play, but we pay dearly for it in terms of self-destructive behaviors.

Seeking Counsel

Personally, I believe we need to "demythologize" this thing called "counseling" and put it back to where it used to be. I have been quite amazed how open and vulnerable men have been with me when we talk over lunch where we are on equal ground, or at some sporting event—which is, again, nonhierarchical turf. Many of the traditional male support places of equality have been taken away, except the local smoke-filled bar. Unfortunately, when men think of "help," they think the only option is professional counseling, which is a very hierarchical relationship. One professional counselor who specializes in men's issues told me that most of the men he sees are what he would classify as the sensitive males who have been rejected by females.

In order for men to walk through adversity better, I believe we need to restore the buddy-system of care. The old hunting or fishing trip, a long walk ruined by eighteen holes of golf, or going to a hockey game together—these are the times when I have found men very open with their pain and willing to ask for help.

As Christian men, we must finally embrace help as a theological concept. It was our asking for help that saved us. Apart from the recognition of our complete inadequacy before God, our eternal destiny would be far different. To believe and fully trust in Jesus as our Savior is the supreme example of why we need to ask for help—*because we really can't help ourselves.*

If these unhealthy ways of dealing with adversity are so common to men, then just doing the opposite might seem like good advice. However, change is never easy. We not only face the adversity, but we must also face the internal obstacles which keep us from adjusting to the adversity.

We'll look at some of those internal barriers now.

For Thought and Discussion

1. On a scale of one to ten, how would you rate yourself on your ability to verbalize feelings? Would your spouse or

best friend agree with your assessment?

2. How have you used the devices of denial, shame, blame, or masking as means of coping during a crisis? Of the four, which have proven most effective in the short term?

3. Can you think of any ill effects that your standard means of coping have produced?

Notes

1. See Shirley M. Smith, "Disaster: Family Disruption in the Wake of Natural Disaster," in *Stress in the Family*, p. 138, where her research suggests "families best able to cope with disaster-caused stresses are those that successfully adjust to normal life crises."

2. Ellis Cose, *A Man's World*, pp. 189–201.

3. Ibid., p. 192.

4. Research by Stephen Johnson, quoted in *A Man's World*, p. 198.

5. Macbeth, Act 4, sc. 3, lines 209–210.

6. Anne Moir and David Jessel, *Brain Sex: The Real Difference Between Men and Women* (New York: Bantam Doubleday, 1989), pp. 47–48.

7. Quoted in *A Man's World*, p. 94.

8. See Warren Farrell's explanation of what women really want, (security) in *Why Men Are the Way They Are* (New York: A Berkley Book, 1988), pp. 24–89.

9. Elie Wiesel, *The Trial of God* (New York: Schocken Books, 1979).

10. John F. Crosby and Nancy L. Jose, "Death: Family Adjustment to Loss," in Figley and McCubbin, *Stress and the Family*, pp. 81–82.

11. Deborah Tannen, *You Just Don't Understand* (New York: Ballentine Books, 1990), pp. 24–25.

Enemies That Defeat Us From Within

I once had an acquaintance who truly was his own worst enemy. It was as if "rejection" was at the core of his being. In every setting, he set himself up as the person who had always been unfairly passed over for promotions and wrongly judged by peers and friends. Over time his "rejected identity" became self-fulfilling prophecy. Even people who liked him and tried to encourage him ended up pulling away from him because of his constantly negative spirit. When they pulled away, it reconfirmed his rejected identity.

Why couldn't he see what he was doing?

It is commonly said of men, "They just don't get the point." Though I don't believe any sin is gender specific, I do believe men have a fatal flaw—very well-honed self-deception devices that cause them to not "get the point"— even in the face of extreme adversity. In Greek tragedies a "fatal flaw" was called *hubris. Hubris*, as Webster defines it, is "a wanton insolence, or arrogance, resulting from excessive pride."

Beneath the normal stress-reactions in a man lurks an insidious enemy. This enemy is *male pride*.

Pride

Originally, *hubris* conveyed the idea that you were invading the space or territory of another. It conveyed the idea of trespass. But to the Greeks *hubris* meant actions and attitudes to which the gods were opposed and upon which they would visit severe retribution.[1] In simple terms, *hubris* was a human attempting to fight against the gods by transgressing their territory. (In most Greek tragedies, the trespasser rarely "got the point" about the resulting retribution!)

In the New Testament a derivative of *hubris*—*hubristes*—is used to describe the man who resists the true God. Paul says these men receive on their own person the due "retribution" for their sinful acts (see Romans 1:30). Here the word is usually translated "insolence," in the sense these men do not get the point as to why they are receiving what they are receiving. So they are angry and resentful toward God. The apostle Paul even confesses that before his conversion he was a *hubristen*—or "insolent violator"—though he acted this way out of ignorance and unbelief.

Likewise, the writer of Hebrews, writing during a time of impending judgment (4:15–16; 10:26; 12:25–28), says, that a man who rejects the Son of God "has insulted the Spirit of grace" (10:29). The word "insulted" here is a form of *hubris*. In other words, the man who rejects the training and discipline of the Son of God under trial stands against God in pride. Therefore he stands pitted against the very grace of God which could help him.

What these passages point to is this: We must face and

overcome our deceptive and dangerous masculine pride which makes us refuse help in adversity.

You would think a book that addresses adversity would be full of sweetness and "comfort." Let me say that I'm genuinely sorry for any man who gets kicked in the head with the frozen boot of life. But I want to talk to you about what you do after the swift, hard kick. I want to talk to you about the heart issue that adversity reveals—that is, the *pride* we all carry.

The pride that wants to remain independent of God is so woven into the fabric of our souls that it mostly goes undetected. Our own hearts deceive us into thinking our intentions are right and good, when a more honest voice inside us says, *"Not so."* Therefore, in adversity it is easy for pride and the noble pain accompanying it to blind us from what God is really doing. This is because self-deceiving hearts make it easy to misread or misinterpret what we think the adversity means.

Let me clarify: I am not saying in every adversity God is sending me some special message. I am of the persuasion that God is in control of all that happens, but I don't believe God necessarily always makes His purposes and meanings clear to me. But adversity *does* show us areas where our security has been wrongly found in our position, possessions, or successful image, and not in God. That's an enormously important *self*-revelation. After all, it takes omniscience to understand all things, and I'm poorly lacking in that attribute! But I can always be sure He is working to cause me to trust and rest in Him more! (see Hebrews).

What I am saying about men and pride is that because of the nature of the fallen human heart, we cannot necessarily trust our *interpretation* of adversity. Pride, lying undetected in our hearts, can lead us to a faulty understanding of what God may be doing.

When I was going through a difficult time in one church ministry, it was far easier to merely blame those making decisions behind my back. Even though they might have been wrong or manipulative, as long as I saw them as the agents of antagonism in my life, I could not see or consider any other option. That's what pride did in my fallen heart.

Pride causes us to place blame where we shouldn't, and wounded pride can also cause us to claim more guilt than we deserve. Some men develop scapegoat mentalities that are unhealthy and in the final analysis reveal a type of concealed pride. On the other hand, the man who quickly assumes he is at fault in any difficulty—or that God is showing him how "unworthy" he is—is not spiritually minded or humble, but filled with a self-focused pride.

Other men can be so self-defeated by adversity that their heart very quickly says "give up" rather than "hang in there." They assume, because their inner inclination is such, that this is God's voice speaking. It may be downright self-deception mixed with a certain lack of courage which the condition of the heart illustrates.

But the biggest internal enemy a man faces is really *himself* and his threatened pride. Let me explain from one of the classic passages about the human heart.

Jeremiah 17:9 says, "The heart is deceitful above all things and beyond cure. Who can understand it?" The Hebrew word for "deceitful" is *'aqov*, and it has the root idea of "grabbing at the heel, or insidiously grasping."[2] The patriarch Jacob was given this term, for his name, *ya'aqov* (Genesis 25:26), because he was grasping his brother's heel on the way out of the womb. The point is fairly clear: Our heart is a deceptive, malicious grasper, and it wants to prevent us from seeing the truth about ourselves. Jeremiah also adds that this condition is never healed. There's no improvement of the natural human heart. Our hearts are so insidiously wounded by the Fall that the resultant self-deception makes it impossible for us, on our own, to accurately access our own condition.

That's why when our wife or boss questions our motive—and lands closer to the truth than we like—we blow up in order to drive them back with our anger.

Jeremiah nails us with the next line, "I the LORD search the heart and examine the mind" (17:10). Only God can know us—and only God can show us the truth about our innermost heart.

Jeremiah's words should both caution men to exercise care when trying to fully understand their adversities. And at the same time, they cause us to recognize our propensity for self-deception. It is quite a terrifying thing for a man to realize that woven into every fabric of his personality and mental processes is a lying spirit within the human heart which he can never really understand on his own. Only by coming, humbled and teachable, to the Lord can we understand the condition of our heart.

To accept our need for full submission to God *in all things*—this is the first step in dealing with *hubris*. Otherwise, we transgress the boundary of God as He does His work in our lives.

Envy

Envy is another serious enemy to our souls when we are going through difficult times. When my marriage is sour, or I don't have a job, or my kids are a mess, or this year was the worst of our lives, we don't get real excited about hearing how well our friends are doing. To do so becomes a breeding ground for envy, and envy is rooted in another fatal flaw—*comparison*.

No matter how spiritually minded a man may be . . . or

think he is . . . envy can cut through his spiritual state like a scalpel. When it cuts, it cuts deep. The resultant tension envy creates can easily lead a man to toss aside his faith.

King David's trusted minister of music confessed how envy led him to almost throw in the spiritual towel. In Psalm 73, Asaph confesses, "Surely God is good to Israel, to those who are pure in heart." (Nice orthodox doctrinal confession!) "But as for me"—that is where my *own* life is at—"my feet had almost slipped; I had nearly lost my foothold" (73:1–2). Asaph admits he had come as close as you can come to falling headlong off the spiritual path. The reason: "For I envied the arrogant when I saw the prosperity of the wicked" (73:3).

Who was this Asaph—the one who was so ready to throw in the towel of faith because of envy? Was he a "baby" Christian, or a "carnal" believer not walking with the Lord, or a man in mid-life crisis? No, he was the writer of many of the psalms, David's chief court musician and choir director. He even stayed on to direct the temple choirs under Solomon and founded a school of music. He was there when the glory of God filled the Solomonic temple. (See 1 Chronicles 16:5–37; 2 Chronicles 5:12–14.) In other words, he had seen it all, done it all. He had been there, done that spiritually.

So why is this godly man—whose job it is to write and sing praises to God—about to capitulate?

If Asaph were alive today, he'd be like some Christians I know whose church or ministry had consumed their life energies and finances. I know men who, like Asaph, look on the prosperity of others and come to the conclusion that serving God isn't "worth it" anymore. They look around them and see others who didn't even care about God, but who are riding on "Easy Street." At the deepest level, they are toying with the idea of writing a resignation notice to God.

In my own life there have been times when I absolutely could not figure out why certain good things were happening to undeserving people. Or on the flip side, why so many bad things were happening to me. I'm sure I'll never fully have an answer, but I am at least encouraged I am not the only man of faith who has ever struggled with such questions. Asaph had experienced far more of the living God than I will ever hope to. And yet for a time he was ready to quit this "godly living" thing.

Envy is like that. It can eat us alive and destroy our faith. It can make us do things we regret later.

The nature of tough times and hard experiences is such that it can surface feelings of envy toward those whose lives look all-together and more prosperous. It is so natural to compare your life with someone else's. But we should never fall for the trap—yes, it's a trap—of comparing our lives to others. Not only does adversity breed comparison, which leads to envy, it also surfaces a bitter rage within men.

Rage

Back during my college days I decided I needed to work in a hospital for the summer. I thought the experience was a good idea since I was a pre-med major with hopes of going on to medical school. I figured I should see if I fainted at the sight of blood before committing myself to this blood-letting field. For one whole summer I filled in for people on vacation at a local hospital.

Weekly, the staff placed me wherever they needed help. Whenever I saw my name listed next to geriatrics, I knew I was in for a long week. As a twenty-year-old, I learned very quickly that men do not die well. At least they didn't at St. Francis Hospital that one summer.

More often than not, these infirm male patients were cantankerous, bitter old men. I learned that the condition of their spirits had nothing to do with their physical ailments. I had seen younger men and children with far more debilitating diseases—but they were often bright-spirited, hopeful, and gracious. Apparently, the bitter souls I encountered had been so soured by someone or something . . . or just life itself . . . that they'd never gotten over it. Now, as they were ailing and dying, they were set on a course to let the rest of humanity know of their deep bitterness.

I can still visualize the sights and sounds of these angry men. What's worse, I see the horrible tendency within myself to join their ranks! How many times have things not gone my way and I start down that slippery road from anger to long-term bitterness?

Psychologists tell us anger is a *secondary* emotion: By that they mean it is the outward response to a more *primary* inner emotion—*hurt*. In this sense, anger is the emotion of pained injustice. It is what we feel when we think life has not been fair. We expect life to be fair and just. It's a part of our native but naive worldview. Christians sometimes hold to it like super glue as a part of their spiritual worldview. We like to believe God will not allow us to go through anything that would seem stressful, hurtful or unjust—in our eyes, that is.

Yet, what do we do with Job? God himself called Job "Blameless and upright, a man who fears God and shuns evil" (Job 1:8). Not a bad assessment for a man to obtain from God! That's what makes the rest of the story so difficult to understand. Job was innocent. And everything that happened to him happened because Satan challenged Job's heart motives before God—in a conversation where Job wasn't even around to defend himself! Job had no clue why he was suffering. By human standards his massive losses were terribly unjust. It's no wonder that Job became angry (Job 15:12–13).

Our rage is rooted in our *expectation* for life to be fair and for God to keep trouble from our door. It's one of our primary assumptions about reality. Whether it's losing a loved one, or being the victim of a violent crime, or finding yourself unemployed, the response is usually the same: Because we did not expect hurt or loss, violence is done to the human spirit. When this happens we rage against the forces that have violated us.

I don't believe those of us who hold to the historic Judeo-Christian faith can honestly believe we are entitled to a singularly pain-free life in this world. We have a benevolent God, but this does not mean we can expect that everything that happens to us in this world will be pleasant. We live in a fallen world where people are called on daily to exercise faith in nonsensical sickness, tragedy, loss, violence, and suffering. We just don't expect it. Or we don't expect it to come to us.

The reason we get so angry is because someone or something we love has been hurt or taken from us. As a result we are wounded. Pain is natural and our anger is then a vivid outpouring of our broken heart.

Whether it is the sudden outburst of anger or just an abiding wrathful spirit, anger is very destructive for men. Though we may have every *reason* to be angry, we must still face the fact that it is destructive to our health, relationships, jobs, children, and marriage. And as hard as it may be to admit, anger is the fleshly reaction to adverse situations (see Galatians 5:19), an emotion that needs to be placed under the control of the Holy Spirit of God.

The apostle Paul had insight into the destructive nature

of bitter anger on our relationships at home. In particular, he admonishes the men not to be embittered with their wives (Colossians 3:19) and not to be embittered toward their children (v. 21). The grief and disappointments caused by adversity can so affect us that we take it out on our wives and children. Paul admonishes us to love our wives and kids, and to stop dumping our bitterness of soul on them. It only spreads the discouragement!

Jim Brady had every reason to become embittered by what life and a gunman had brought upon him. Being paralyzed by a .22-calibre bullet meant for President Reagan, Brady faced, and is still facing, years of difficult therapy. He will never be normal again. But in his own words, he said he vented his anger on his physical therapists, entering into an antagonistic competition with them to show them every day he could do more. He said, "Quitting has not entered my mind."[3] A good word to the wise!

Guilty Conscience

Andy was a delightful guy. I really liked him. But every so often, he and his wife would get into one of those century-old arguments that never gets finished. Then Andy would explode and pop her one. As a result, she would end up in my office. I would call him in, and he'd always be the first to apologize and say it would never happen again. Months would go by and then it would happen again. Same routine.

After one session with his wife, as she was walking out the office door she turned around and said, "Andy was never the same after Vietnam!" I couldn't believe what I heard. I had known this couple for years, and had them in for counseling numerous times. Yet they had never revealed—nor had I ever asked—about military service or wartime experience. A light bulb went on in my head. *Andy's a vet. Could he be dealing with posttraumatic stress symptoms?*

During my next time with Andy, he gradually began to open a new window into his soul. He had massive guilt about what he had done in Vietnam. A guilty conscience was preventing him from making peace with the incredible internal adversity that had left him in turmoil since the early 1970s!

Over lunch, he finally responded to my probing about his wartime experience. He looked at me and said, "Tell me something, Chaplain, why is it that now—some twenty-five years later—I can still feel the pleasure of killing those *gooks* and cutting off their body parts?"

Few men ever get this honest about what really happened over there. Most wives don't ask about it, or even want to know. Therefore, the strangely pleasurable thrills of war—whether it's knowing your planes have successfully bombed a city, or darker things such as Andy's experience—can get buried in a man's soul. Only to haunt him much later as a reminder of how "sick" he must be. War breeds this condition. Few understand it. The demon Andy had lived with for a quarter of a century was guilt—true moral guilt.

The psychological community during the Freudian era did not believe in true moral guilt. Guilt was just repressed sexuality, or the result of being raised with too strict a social code. But the kind of guilt Andy was experiencing could not be minimized, reasoned, or psychoanalyzed away. Now, I don't want to oversimplify the problem of guilt. There are many men who punish themselves for reasons other than a conscience riddled with true guilt. But committing barbaric acts against the body of another human being, in my opinion, produces clear moral guilt. Most in the mental health community have no idea how to handle this. Shortly after Vietnam, the professional answer to "guilty vets" was that they were serving their country and following orders, and therefore they should not feel guilty. Unfortunately, many of them *did* feel guilty. So since society did not punish or correct them for their crimes, they began to self-punish. Many have punished themselves with drugs and alcohol. Many have destroyed relationships. Some have wound up as suicides. Chaim Shatan, founder of the Vietnam Veterans Work Group, writes,

> Veterans will often ask, "How do we turn off the guilt?" "Can we atone?" . . . their own answers follow quickly: they speak of "paying their dues" for surviving unscathed when others did not survive. They invite self-punishment by picking self-defeating fights, inviting rejection from near ones, even getting involved in a remarkably high number of single-car, single-occupant accidents.[4]

What fascinates me about this quote is the number of theological terms Shatan uses. Terms like "atone" and "punish" are on the lips of those who have committed moral wrongs. In some mysterious way, this is the natural response within the human soul about moral wrongs. We instinctively know that moral crimes demand punishment and some form of atonement.

In the absence of an atonement from without—that is, the substitutionary atonement of Jesus Christ—we create our own atonements. What every man who has violated moral law needs is atonement—not from *within* but from *without*. This is precisely why Jesus Christ died. In the words of Isaiah, the Messiah "was crushed for our iniquities; the punishment that brought us peace was upon him, and by his wounds we are healed" (Isaiah 53:5).

Even men in everyday environments—like business, politics, and professional life—can do unthinkable things which wrong people in their path. Chuck Colson has often mused that almost all indicted in the Watergate fiasco were attorneys who were highly trained in the law. As we noted in Chapter 3, being an innocent victim is not the reason that some men are unable to cope with adversity. We can do or say things that wrong or in some way destroy another human being. Afterward, we can fall into a cycle of self-punishment in an attempt to atone for our crimes, or we resort to addiction to deaden the pain of tormenting guilt. In this sense, a guilty conscience can become a terrible enemy to our souls.

I need to add an important point here to the story I told earlier about Andy and his wife. If you assumed that he was not a Christian, you were wrong. In fact, Andy was a very committed Christian and an active churchgoer. Even though he had asked Jesus Christ to be his Savior and claimed His forgiveness, Andy had never placed his Vietnam experience under the light of the Cross. As we talked, it eventually came out that Andy believed—at a deep level—that because of what he had done in Vietnam, Christ could never find him acceptable. No wonder he could not be released from his internal guilt. No wonder that over time he'd developed a pattern of rejecting the very people who loved him.

The first step in helping Andy was to help him recognize that his guilt-based belief was in essence denying the finished work of Christ. As shocking as it was to him, I had to point out his emotional denial was tantamount to denying that Christ's death was powerful enough to fully forgive his sins. In other words he was denying Christ!

Next, I tried to have him reframe his Vietnam experience in the sense that Christ was very present in those dark

jungles and in fact had seen everything that happened. Yet
Christ had still taken the punishment for Andy's crimes.
For my friend, I prayed with the apostle Paul. "May he
strengthen your hearts so that you will be blameless [Greek,
amemptos, or "not guilty"] and holy in the presence of our
God and Father when our Lord Jesus comes with all his
holy ones" (1 Thessalonians 3:13).

Fear and Mistrust

In the death-dealing jungles of Vietnam, every soldier
fought battles with his own personal fears. If he was in his
right mind, his fear was healthy. Besides, he was rarely in
the rice paddies alone. There was always someone protecting your back. You were afraid, but you were not alone.

But upon returning home, the nature of the warfare
changed. The anti-war movement labeled vets "baby kill-
ers" and "warmongers." To wear the uniform in public was
to bring disgrace upon yourself or, worse, be spat on. The
emotional irony that existed for these vets was that they
were now having to trade the "safety and security" of a
trusted environment for one in America which was fearful
and rejecting. No one wanted to hear their "war stories,"
which has always been the male way of processing feelings
and giving their wartime experiences positive meaning.
Farrell observes rightly, "Deprived of war stories to reframe
their fears and affirm themselves, they were, instead, overwhelmed by their fears and overwhelmed by self-doubt."[5]

Deep-seated mistrust and suspicion of other men—
wherever it comes from—creates an emotional and mental
wall between a man going through a trial and other men
who could potentially help him. One man confided in me
that as a result of seeing his church torn apart by power
plays between the board and the pastor, "I will never trust

the leadership in a church again." On a more personal note, I was once in a situation where I had extreme pressure to perform at work and was getting constant criticism. I knew I needed to talk to someone about the work situation. But who? I finally came up with the name of a man who had previously worked for the same organization and knew all the players in leadership. Over lunch, I asked him, "Who can I trust in this organization?" There was silence for several minutes, and then his curt reply, "I wouldn't trust anyone there with my *dog*."

Fear and *mistrust* among men take away the most powerful resource when dealing with adversity . . . the understanding and acceptance of another man. Without this we find ourselves in the trenches of life all alone, with no one protecting our backs.

Over the last five years, I have crisscrossed the country speaking at men's conferences and retreats. I have participated in small groups with men and have had extensive exposure to men in the military. During these times, some men have risked potential rejection and misunderstanding and have gotten brutally honest about their fears. One thing always emerges: They are terribly fearful of being viewed as a loser by others—not only by male friends but by women, and especially their own wives.

I had met Tom at his high-rise office in center-city Philadelphia. As we exited the office building on our way to lunch, we turned a corner and lying in front of us was a homeless man begging on the sidewalk. We both just kept talking and sort of played as though we didn't see him. (As Christians, if we really saw him, we might have to do something!) A few minutes down the sidewalk, my friend turned to me and said, "You know, that's my worst fear."

"What?" I innocently replied.

"That guy back there—homeless and poor."

I tried to keep from laughing, knowing that my friend was vice president of a multinational company. But underneath my humorous tone, I had to admit I had often had the same thoughts.

Maybe we have never recovered from high school. If we were successful jocks, we were automatically placed in the "in group"—but there was a gnawing fear that the success would be short-lived. One injury, or graduation, would end our success, and we would again be relegated to the "loser" category. Even though, as fifty-year-old men, some guys have assets that are mind-blowing, many still see themselves as eighth-grade losers, one failure away from begging on the street.

I am convinced when men face adversity it is *fear* of becoming a "loser" that causes them to make some very dumb decisions. They take out high-interest loans, get into bad relationships, take a second mortgage on the family house, or have a romantic affair with someone who makes them not feel like a loser. All this to maintain the illusion of a successful self-image.

Love Lost

Why is this the case? I believe our fear of failure is connected to a more fundamental one: *our fear of losing love.*

In the men's groups I have been in, we eventually get around to discussing our work-related difficulties. When I ask other men if they've ever shared their work problems with their wives, most just mumble something unintelligible—which means, "No, I really haven't." We can be going through great difficulties at work, but when we come home at night and our wives ask about our day we would rather say, "Everything is fine"—even if it's a total lie. To women, this is grossly dishonest. But many men think of it

as "protection" and "care." They desire to protect their
wives from the insecurity that would be bred by their honesty. Therefore, the facade of "okayness" prevents men
from seeking or asking for help.

Farrell explains the dilemma.

> The "Suicide Class" is 91 percent white, usually
> well educated, and at least middle class. They are the
> "Success Class." Or at least they were until they lost
> their job or their savings. But why suicide when I've
> been saying it's feeling not being loved or needed that's
> the catalyst? Because the men who are successful have
> become the most dependent on success to attract *love*.
> When this man loses his success, he often fears he will
> lose love.[6]

So fearing the loss of love and respect from our wives,
most of us keep our worst fears tightly bound within us. We
work hard to preserve an illusion of security, hoping it will
ensure that our wives will continue to love us.

I wish this relational "side-step" dance could only be
said of men outside the faith. In my experience, I have seen
the same dynamic of dishonesty at work in the lives of the
most deeply committed Christian men. Pastors stay in hor-
ribly conflicted ministries in order to keep providing an in-
come for their families. Professionals who long to become
artists, or anything else, stay in "boring" jobs for fear of losing their wives' validation of them as men and good providers.

And so fear can also prevent men from handling life's
adversity with integrity and confidence.

In some men these internal enemies are so firmly rooted
and disguised that their presence goes unnoticed and unex-
amined. Of course men who are more reflective know all
too well that these are the enemies of our souls. Even so,

they continue to be enemies until we begin to think differently about the role of difficulties in our lives. In the next chapter, we will look at a "God's-eye" view of adversity in contrast with our own.

Not until we recognize what God is doing in adversity can we begin to break free from our bondage to these enemies within.

For Thought and Discussion

1. In your own life, where have you seen pride, envy, anger, guilt, or fear sabotage your own best efforts?
2. From the list of internal enemies above, with which ones do you struggle the most?
3. Are there some other self-destructive enemies you see in your own life that are not mentioned in this chapter?

Notes

1. *Theological Dictionary of the New Testament*, Vol. 8, Gerhard Kittel, ed. (Grand Rapids: Eerdmans, 1985), pp. 295–307.
2. *Hebrew and English Lexicon of the Old Testament*, Brown, Drive and Briggs (Oxford), p. 784.
3. Dennis Wholey, *When the Worst That Can Happen Already Has* (New York: Berkley Books, 1992), p. 46.
4. Chaim F. Shatan, "Stress Disorders Among Vietnam Veterans: The Emotional Context of Combat Continues," in Charles R. Figley, ed., *Stress Disorders Among Vietnam Veterans* (New York: Brunner/Mazel, 1978), p. 48.
5. Warren Farrell, *The Myth of Male Power*, p. 145.
6. Ibid., p. 172.

God's View of Adversity and Ours

One of those rare occasions when the dust in my study finally got to me (you know, the maid just never shows up), I decided to do something about it. I got up and began dusting bookshelves, lamps, and pictures on the wall. While removing the dusty accumulation from one picture, the nail came loose, and the picture went crashing to the floor. The frame and glass shattered into hundreds of irreparable pieces. This experience resembles what happens in adversity.

As idealistic humans we carry around a picture in our heads of how we think life should be, a portrait of our ideal world. It's painted with ideals we rarely think about or articulate. For the most part, we don't even know they exist—until adversity hits. Then our assumptive world falls and shatters. We no longer know how to frame our experience, because the frame itself is broken.

The issue I want to raise in this chapter is how God looks upon our ideal pictures of life and the surrounding framework of our assumptions.

What Happens in Adversity: The Human Frame

Anyone who has raised teenagers knows there is something about testosterone and estrogen kicking in that convinces teens they're invulnerable. I'm not sure why this is, or exactly where it comes from, but researchers have confirmed that when we reach adulthood we have a fundamental assumption of invulnerability. It usually begins in adolescence and stays with us throughout our adult life.

One authority writes, "Whether we like it or not, each of us, because he has a human brain, forms a theory of reality that brings order into an otherwise chaotic world of experience. We need a theory to make sense out of the world."[1] We know bad things happen in the world, even in our own community. The nightly news reminds us of such grim realities. But when we get up in the morning, we have the expectation we will get to work without accident, harm, or a heart attack. That's our assumption of invulnerability at work. We don't think about it—it's just there. (In fact, the person who compulsively thinks about how vulnerable he is, we label as "sick" or "paranoid.") Janoff-Bulman comments, "People overestimate the likelihood of their experiencing positive outcomes in life and underestimate the likelihood of experiencing negative events."[2]

It's true. When I get on an airplane, I expect to arrive safely where I am going and on time. When my wife goes to the store, I expect her to go, do her shopping, and return unharmed. When I launch my kids into the adult world, I don't expect them to be poor, raped, mutilated, hurt, diseased, or divorced. This is all a part of our assumptive world, which translates into a view of reality that's free from harm and vulnerability.

Is this really the way God looks at our lives? Is this the

worldview that the Bible offers us?

We Americans seem to have this "trouble-free life" assumption rooted in our mental processes. Now rationality is among our greatest gifts. But when adversity comes out of nowhere, this gift becomes a curse. Our rational processes turn in full force *against* the source of confusion or pain. As rational beings we assume, secondly, that everything should make sense. Assuming we can or should understand everything that happens to us is deeply rooted in our inner mental processes. As men we use reason to figure out almost everything—as opposed to women who tend to have more intuitive strengths.[3] We try to find the rationale in the adversity. But adversity shatters and challenges our rational mind. When a man can no longer figure something out, or see the *why* in the event, part of his assumptive world is shattered and dies.

Bard and Sangrey have observed, "If the world doesn't make sense, people can't do anything with confidence."[4] Fundamental to the human condition is the experience that we do not want to believe things happen randomly. Therefore, instinctively we seek the meaning in the adversity. Nazi death-camp survivor, Viktor Frankl, affirmed, "In some way, suffering ceases to be suffering at the moment it finds a meaning."[5]

If we naturally expect life to be rational and make sense, what happens when adversity strikes unexpectedly and we can't see any meaning in it? Again, I raise the question from God's perspective: We are rational creatures—but does this mean we should be able to understand everything, including adversity? Should we try to control life by trying to see a reason in everything?

The third assumption has been referred to earlier. This is the assumption of morality—that we live, or *should* live, in a just and fair world. If I were God I know how I would run the world. I would sit in my heavenly domain and look down upon all those who really love me and are trying to live for me. I would be so pleased with them, I would bestow unique blessings on their lives. I would allow the right amount of rain to fall on their crops, I would give them good health and let them find gold, silver, and oil on their property. I would make sure all their children grow up to love and honor me as well. But upon the others—those who curse my name and have nothing to do with me, who live completely corrupt lives—I would throw upon them earthquakes, hurricanes, tornados, poverty, joblessness, cancer, and HIV. That would be just and fair! I would be a just and fair God.

Most of us do carry the assumption that God should run the world somewhat like this, in a way that makes sense in our eyes. We expect to be rewarded for our goodness and to have the bad guys punished. The expectation for life to be fair is one of the primary assumptions that frames reality for us. What's worse, we can quote passages about God's justice and fairness. (See Psalm 7:9; Isaiah 45:21; Zechariah 9:9; Revelation 15:3.) We can sing, "Just and true are your ways, Oh, Lord"—but our souls vent another tune.

Honest spirits find themselves singing, "Unjust and unfair are your ways!" Assuming we *should* live in a moral universe is what slays us during times of crisis and adversity. And conclusions some draw from their pain make matters even worse.

As a Result . . .

Over the years, I have noticed how both men and women sometimes radically alter their behavior after a crisis. A man is told he has cancer, and suddenly he goes on a spending spree or becomes uncharacteristically promis-

cuous. A woman who's been abandoned by her husband becomes so disillusioned with life, she no longer wants the
custody or care of her children. The logic is simple. If you
expect life to be just and fair, and it turns out not to be, then
what's the point of morality? If a moral universe is a joke,
then why not do anything? Morality talk becomes mean-
ingless. So goes the (often unconscious) logic of the sufferer.

Adversity can provide a wake-up call about who we
really are. Once a man sees himself as powerless to change
something, or is helpless in the face of forces beyond his
control, his self-perception becomes severely challenged if
not shattered. And the assumption we carry about who we
are can be very powerful. The change from a competent, all-
together man to a powerless, victimized-by-circumstances
kind of man is too extreme for some men.

One Israeli researcher, studying war vets, notes, "The
traumatic experience . . . cannot be integrated into the structure of self and meaning, and thus hinders the continuance
of the autonomous functions of the structure."[6] This means
the sense of wholeness and integration we have within ourselves about who we are is destroyed. The new face that
looks back at me from the mirror is no longer me but someone
else. A man might say to himself, "Being a victim is not me.
Feeling virtually incompetent is not me. But then who am I?"
To not know who you are in the middle of adversity is often
worse than the adversity itself. In short, we lose our bearings,
our boundaries, and a sense of who we are. "The central fea-
ture of the experience is the final horrible 'realization' that
the rules that define the individual's identity and reality are
not operational anymore."[7]

Notice on the chart "Circle of Assumptions,"[8] how adversity challenges each of these fundamental human assumptions. A man with a competent self-image now

Circle of Assumptions

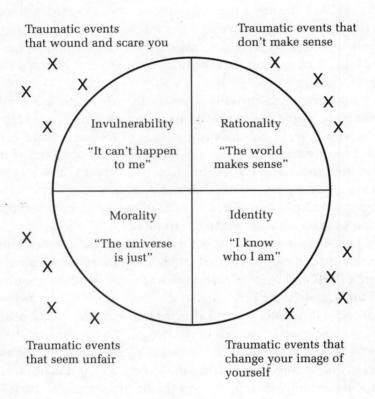

Traumatic events
that wound and scare you

Traumatic events that
don't make sense

Invulnerability

"It can't happen
to me"

Rationality

"The world
makes sense"

Morality

"The universe
is just"

Identity

"I know
who I am"

Traumatic events
that seem unfair

Traumatic events that
change your image of
yourself

struggles with self-identity—and life which once seemed
just, fair, and meaningful, now seems very unfair and irra-
tional. For the first time, this man may have developed an
acute scary sense of vulnerability.

Having looked at the human side of adversity, I ask,
"How true are these basic human assumptions as compared
to a more biblical view?" Or how does God look upon the
experience of human adversity?

What Happens in Adversity: God's Point of View

To say we can know God's specific intentions in adversity is probably an absurd statement. But what we'll do in the rest of this chapter and the next is to look at biblical teachings in order to gain a God's-eye-view on adversity. Fortunately, we are not left in complete darkness on the subject, but have the light of divine insight as revealed in the Holy Scriptures. But the perspective we find there will still be distorted by our own spiritual eyesight problems and the fact that God has not yet revealed all of himself nor all of His plan to us.

When it comes to understanding adversity, we are like Moses wanting to see God's face. In response, God allowed Moses only a small glimpse of His back (see Exodus 33:23). To see God's *purposes* face-to-face is something He apparently has not chosen to reveal to us, and I'm not sure we could see them and live. So we must settle for a glimpse.

Adversity and God's Judgment

I was once speaking at a state university and was able to mention God's name without being thrown out. As soon as I was finished a student came up and said, "How can you believe in a God who allowed six million Jews to be slaughtered in Nazi Germany?"

Since there were other students standing around, I really didn't want to get into the various theological and philosophical means used to acquit God of such charges. I answered, "If you don't have God to believe in, what *do* you have to believe in?"

The student snapped back, "What's wrong with believing in man?"

I replied, "Wasn't it men who killed six million Jews?"

As Rabbi Telushkin has said, "What happened at Auschwitz might make belief in God difficult for some people, but for me it makes belief in man even more difficult. It was man, not God, who built Auschwitz."[9]

Sometimes while channel-surfing through the cable networks, I stumble across The Learning Channel. I usually get hooked by some wildlife program. I quickly fall in love with a young, adorable antelope with all its playful antics. But then the camera pans to the stalking lioness. With lightning speed the hunter strikes and kills the antelope for the sake of her own adorable cubs. Even at the insect level, the story is the same. Big insects eat smaller ones, and larger ones eat the big ones—then a bird swoops down and eats the largest one! The story of nature is one of both macro and micro violence. Philosopher John Stuart Mill bluntly observes,

> Nature impales men, breaks them as if on the wheel, casts them to be devoured by wild beasts, burns them to death, crushes them with stones, starves them with hunger, freezes them with cold, poisons them by the quick or slow venom of her exhalations, and has hundreds of other hideous deaths in reserve.[10]

Nature is cruel.

To look at the global human situation is to be confronted with the unexplainable magnitude of both human and natural violence. What light does Scripture shed on this accumulated mass of human adversity?

In Lebanon today there is a Syrian-backed terrorist group called Hamas. Their specialty is well planned, ingeniously coordinated terrorist attacks on unsuspecting civilians living in countries supportive of Israel. Ironically, their name has the same spelling as the Hebrew word for "violence," a catch-all term used in the Bible for all kinds of adversity. It doesn't take long for human violence to appear in the biblical story. Out of jealousy, Cain kills his brother, and as a result the earth has its first taste of human blood (see Genesis 4:5, 10). Seth, Abel's replacement, is conceived, and the commentary tells us he is made in the image of his fallen father, Adam (Genesis 5:1–2). Cain is then cursed from the place where his brother's blood was spilled (4:11), and the rest of humanity follows in the nature of their fallen father (Romans 5:19). As the population increases, so violence grows proportionally (Genesis 6:1, 5–6). God looks upon His creation and grieves, being filled with pain (6:6). Mankind had become so corrupt God declares the entire earth *hamas*—violent (8:11). If one family had not been preserved, human history as we know it would not exist. Noah, fortunately, found grace in the eyes of God (6:8).

From this look at early biblical history, it is clear where adversity has its roots. Adversity is the result of God's judgment upon the first couple who transgressed the line between divine liberty and prohibition. All creation falls.

In short, *hamas*, or violence, becomes the subtext of both human and natural history. In the Psalms, David fears being turned over to his enemies who breath out "violence" (Psalm 27:12). Narrative passages depict *hamas* as massive blood-letting (Judges 9:24), destruction of natural habitat (Habakkuk 2:17), and violence consuming entire cities and countries (Ezekiel 7:23; 8:17). A man's mouth is even said to create violence (Proverbs 10:6). One scholar summarizes *hamas* as the "cold-blooded and unscrupulous infringement of the personal rights of others, motivated by greed and hate and often making use of physical violence and brutality."[11]

If adversity is the product of God's judgment on fallen

mankind, a study of *hamas* also reveals how men respond to being victims of violence. In the Psalms, *hamas* is what the psalmist cries out at, his unjust treatment and numerous afflictions. David petitions God: "Look upon my affliction and my distress. . . . See how my enemies have increased and how fiercely [*hamas*] they hate me" (Psalm 25:18–19). As he looks upon the inhabitants of Jerusalem, he prays, "Confuse the wicked, O Lord, confound their speech, for I see violence [*hamas*] and strife in the city" (Psalm 55:9). After suffering massive personal losses, Job accuses God of violence. He utters, "God has wronged me and drawn his net around me. Though I cry, violence [*hamas*], I get no response; though I call for help, there is no justice" (Job 19:6–7).

What the above passages illustrate is that God does not play games with us about adversity. Violence is a part of human history since it is rooted in human hearts. Violence is so woven into the fabric of fallen human society and nature, and it cannot be plucked out, eradicated, ignored, outlawed, or spiritualized away.

At God's Side

Perhaps the first glimpse we gain of God's view of adversity is that He sees it for what it really is—that is, *violence* that's the by-product of the sinful fall. God knows we live in a fallen world where suffering and violence exist— and without diminishing its force, *He meets us face-to-face within the darkness of the human dilemma.* He will walk with us as we rebuild our world and our view of ourselves.

As we are coming to see things from God's view, coming to stand on His side, we will need to recognize that there is another player in the story. God's view of adversity is not complete without looking at the great *antagonist* of the universe. That's where we'll turn next.

For Thought and Discussion

1. Reflect for a moment where in your life you have seen your worldview collapse. Even for a few days, or hours.
2. Of the four shattered pieces of one's worldview (invulnerability, rationality, morality, and self-identity), which has been most affected by adversity in your own life?
3. How do you react to God being "behind" adversity? Does this make God the originator of evil? Does it change the nature of the adversity to say God is the "architect" of evil without being the personal "author" or "agent" of the evil?

Notes

1. S. Epstein, "The Self Concept Revisited," *American Psychologist*, Vol. 28 (1973), pp. 404–416.
2. Ronnie Janoff-Bulman, "The Aftermath of Victimization: Rebuilding Shattered Assumptions," in Charles R. Figley, *Trauma and Its Wake* (New York: Brunner-Mazel), p. 19.
3. See Moir and Jessel, *Brain Sex*, chapter on "The Ability Gap" for these differences (New York: Dell Publishing Co., 1992), pp. 88–98.
4. Bard and Sangrey, *The Crime Victim's Book* (New York: Carol Publishing Group, 1986), p. 54.
5. Viktor E. Frankl, *Man's Search for Meaning* (New York: Washington Square Press, 1984), p. 135.
6. Ben Yakar, "The Collapse of a Structure: A Structural Approach to Trauma," *Journal of Traumatic Stress*, Vol. 2 (1989), p. 437.

7. Ibid., p. 442.

8. Robert Hicks, *Failure to Scream* (Nashville: Thomas Nelson, 1993), p. 17.

9. Rabbi Joseph Telushkin, "Why Does God Allow Such Things," in Dennis Wholey, *When the Worst That Can Happen Already Has* (New York: Berkley Publishing, 1993), p. 106.

10. Routledge and Kegan Paul, eds., John Stuart Mill, *Essays of Ethics, Religion and Society*, Vol. 10, *The Collected Works of John Stuart Mill* (Toronto: University of Toronto, 1969), p. 385.

11. Word study by H. Haag, in *Theological Dictionary of the Old Testament*, Vol. IV, G. Johannes Botterweck and Helmer Ringgren, eds. (Grand Rapids: Eerdmans, 1980), p. 482.

How God Looks Upon Adversity:
Light in the Midst of Darkness

The apostle Paul was probably one of the most spiritually minded men in the Bible. Amazing, since his life was filled with hardship. In offering his credentials of apostleship to a suspicious church he writes,

> Five times I received from the Jews the forty lashes minus one. Three times I was beaten with rods, once I was stoned, three times I was shipwrecked, I spent a night and a day in the open sea, I have been constantly on the move, I have been in danger from rivers, in danger from bandits, in danger from my own countrymen, in danger from Gentiles; in danger in the city, in danger in the country, in danger at sea; and in danger from false brothers. I have labored and toiled and have often gone without sleep; I have known hunger and thirst and have often gone without food; I have been cold and naked. Besides everything else, I face daily the pressures of my concern for all the churches (2 Corinthians 11:24–28).

In spite of these overwhelming adversities, when Paul reflects on the nature of all he faced, he places the realm of warfare beyond mere human forces. Paul knew that ship captains, prison guards, bandits, false brothers, or the lack of food, drink, and clothing were not his *real* enemies. His enemies, and ours, are the spiritual forces of evil.

"For our struggle is not against flesh and blood," wrote Paul, "but against the rulers, against the authorities, against the powers of this dark world, against the spiritual forces of evil in the heavenly realms. Therefore, put on the full armor of God" (Ephesians 6:12–13). This biblical insight is crucial for obtaining a divine perspective on adversity. Trouble usually hits us through the agency of some human or natural disaster. However, Paul exhorts us to *look beyond* the human situation to see the real adversary who wants to use the outward circumstance to destroy us from within.

If our real opponent is Satan, then Jesus' words about his character is accurate: He is a murderer and destroyer, and no element of truth resides in his character. He will use the truth and quote the truth, but only in attempt to pull the brethren away from the truth about God (see John 8:44).

In the biblical narrative the word "satan" and its derivatives are used to describe: those who oppose David's rule (Psalm 38:19; 109:4; 2 Samuel 19:22); and Solomon's reign (1 Kings 11:14, 23, 25). It is Satan who incites David to number his army (1 Chronicles 21:1); Satan accuses Joshua, the high priest, before the angel of the Lord (Zechariah 3:10); and it is a satanic spirit that goes out to make the prophets of God speak wrongly (1 Kings 22:19–22).

In the New Testament, this opposer is still alive and well, although apparently he knows he is a defeated foe (John 12:31; 16:11). He puts thoughts of betrayal into the mind of Judas (John 13:2). Peter calls him a "roaring lion" looking for someone to devour (1 Peter 5:8).

When pain and confusion strike, Satan has his greatest opportunity. How easy it is for us to entertain accusations of God when we're feeling crushed and abandoned.

Hear me out. I am not one who sees some demon in every circumstance and human vice. But I do believe behind every adversity stands the Chief Adversary of God, who would like to use our troubles to destroy our faith in the Father. This is why the apostle can say, "We do not wrestle against flesh and blood." No matter what kind of adversity I face, Satan's desire is to see me destroyed by it.

Knowing this alerts me to the kind of warfare I must then wage. I must utilize spiritual resources to defeat this enemy of the spirit realm (2 Corinthians 10:4). It's important to see adversity from God's perspective—to see the spiritual warfare aspect of our troubles. It raises an even more difficult question, though. Has God left us exclusively to the designs of Satan—or does He have other purposes for adversity?

Adversity as Trial

When I served as coordinating chaplain for the Delta 191 crash, I was quite amazed by the response of the victims' family members and survivors. Almost every person asked the same question: "Why," and "Why, God?"

Adversity very quickly raises the question of God's involvement no matter what the religious viewpoint of the sufferer. On any flight today there will be on board Buddhists, Hindus, Jews, Catholics, born-again Christians, atheists, and agnostics. But in my case, everyone on flight 191 asked the same question, "Why did God allow this to happen?" They didn't question, "Why did Mother Nature allow this to happen?" or pray to their Universal Impersonal Source of Enlightenment. They didn't even ask, "Why did Satan do this?" They simply connected the tragedy with God.

No, the reality that we live in a fallen world where Satan can still create havoc is not the first utterance on our lips when we encounter trouble. Planted within our conscience is the human connection we make between God and adversity. As Elie Wiesel put it, "A Jew may love God, or he may fight God, but he can't ignore God."[1] Again, the Scriptures have much to say in this regard.

God actively permits Satan to test Job (1:9, 12; 2:1–5). In fact, it is God who first raises the issue of Job's immaculate character to Satan (1:8; 2:3). Twice God probes, "Have you considered my servant Job?" My response to this if I were Job would be, "Thanks a lot, God!"

Once the testing has started, God actively limits the parameters in which Satan can function. He will not allow Satan to take the life of Job (2:6), though God permits his flesh to suffer. In other words, behind the harmful purposes Satan enjoys is the limiting control of God. But what purposes does God have in allowing such suffering? For Job the passage is clear. God wanted Satan to learn that Job would remain faithful in his integrity before God even though he was severely tested—and maybe He wanted Job to see that too (2:3).

Other biblical instances are not as clear. When Satan incited David to number his armed men (1 Chronicles 21:1), the parallel passage in the Samuel narrative says, "The anger of the Lord burned against Israel, and he incited David against them, saying, 'Go and count Israel and Judah' " (2 Samuel 24:1). Behind Satan's agency in David's life is this unexplainable anger of the Lord against Israel which causes David to do what he did.

In passages like these, it's hard to separate what God

does from what Satan does. But one thing is clear. God *does* bring about trials in order to test the believer's faithfulness to Him. This is what happened with Abraham. The command to Abram was, "Take your son, your only son Isaac. . . . Sacrifice him there as a burnt offering" (Genesis 22:2). This was Abram's trial of fire. Likewise, with Moses at the waters of Marah (Exodus 15:25), and in the giving of the Law (Exodus 20:1–20), God places His sons under a test. One scholar argues, "When the Old Testament speaks of Yahweh testing His covenant son, it means that God arranges a test to find out whether His son is true to the covenant."[2]

The Hebrew concept of "test"—*nasah*—carries over into the New Testament in the Greek word *peirasomos*—translated as "tempt, test, or approve."[3] Without commenting on the source of testing, Peter acknowledges that the suffering Christians are facing is a trial of their faith (1 Peter 1:6–7) and a sharing in the sufferings of the Messiah (1 Peter 4:12–13). Satan can also tempt (*peiraze*—verbal form) a man during sexual abstinence from his wife (1 Corinthians 7:5–6), or during persecutions (1 Thessalonians 2:14–16; 3:5).

Satan can also use erring brothers to tempt the faithful (Galatians 6:1). Paul also reveals that his "thorn in the flesh" is a "messenger of Satan" (2 Corinthians 12:7). But the most difficult passage on this topic is the one found in James. Here the writer tries to distance the concept of testings from having their origin in God. He says, "When tempted"—*peirazomenos*—"no one should say, 'God is tempting me' "—*peirazomai*—"for God cannot be tempted by evil"—*apeirastos*—"nor does he tempt anyone"—*peirzei*. Here, James roots the source of testing in human lust and desire (1:12–15).

So how can these passages be reconciled? On the one

hand, it is God who brings the test, while on the other hand, James says we are tested by our own natural desires.

My view is that God *is* the author of trials and that He uses them to reveal the true content of our souls in order to develop spiritual purity, honesty, and faith. We can talk glibly about "spiritual growth" and "character development," but the only thing I have found that produces real Christlikeness is *trials.*

That's why Scripture instructs us to welcome trials with a joyous response (see James 1:2–4; 1 Peter 1:7). I believe it's theologically consistent to view God as testing us, His sons within the covenant relationship He has established with us. Once we understand this role of testing, we should be concerned if we are not facing some kind of adversity— for it's *through* adversity that our souls are purified and we have a chance to share in God's holiness.

Adversity as Mystery

I started the last chapter by admitting my lack of ability to understand adversity fully from the divine perspective. At this point, I must reaffirm my deficiency. Much about adversity is lost to us in the mysterious purposes of God. This means a final understanding as to why something happens may be without a satisfactory answer. Perhaps this final insight will illustrate why this is the case.

Adversity is a mystery because of the freedom of God and the relative freedom of men. God, as the only wise and absolutely free being, decides what He is going to do without consulting His creation—namely us! (See Isaiah 46:8– 11; Exodus 33:19; Romans 11:33.) His intentions are beyond us in the final analysis. At the same time, the Scriptures present mankind as making free decisions based on their own limited insight, mostly based on selfish desires.

Joseph's experience, for instance, demonstrates the maliciously free decisions of Joseph's brothers, Potiphar, and Pharaoh to harm Joseph (Genesis 50:20). The mystery is found in that "God intended it for good."

The mystery of adversity lies in how God brings together the free malicious actions of Satan, men, and nature to fulfill His own purposes. As Solomon concludes, "Many are the plans in a man's heart, but it is the Lord's purpose that prevails" (Proverbs 19:21).

There is a second element to this mystery. When we encounter adversity we are often standing on the threshold of wonder—perhaps awake enough for the first time to witness some of the most mysteriously extraordinary works of God.

After Israel's redemption at the Red Sea, Moses sang unto the Lord, "Who is like You—majestic in holiness, awesome in glory, working wonders?" (Exodus 15:11). The word translated "wonders"—*pele*—carries the ideas of the unusual and extraordinary, things which are beyond human capabilities and comprehension.[4] It is for these extraordinary works the psalmist and prophets consistently praise God (Psalm 78:11; Isaiah 25:1).

But "wonders" also bring to bear the reality that there are many things we humans just cannot know. King David admitted in all humility there were some things too *pele* to be adequately understood. As a result he did not concern himself with them (Psalm 131:1). Agar glories in his "deficiency" in understanding the ways of snakes, eagles, ships, and the way of a man with a maiden! (Proverbs 30:18–19). Job, likewise, confesses his wrong in trying to understand and speak of things too *pele* for him to know (Job 42:3).

Part of the mysteriously wonderful nature of God is that the adversity He allows often creates final outcomes too *pele*—too wonderful—for us to understand. When we confront such things, all we can do is fall on our face and worship God for the mystery and wonder of God revealed out of adversity.

In My Lap

Recently, I experienced just such a mystery. For many months it seemed like my employment was "on the line" due to the collapse of a foundation in which my seminary had placed funds. My wife and I had worried, prayed, tried to find other employment as "plan B," all to no avail. Without dreaming I could be accepted as a reservist, I applied to one of the air force professional education schools—a paying job for ten months. Two weeks before I received my "pink slip" from the seminary, my acceptance letter came from the air force.

God in His mysterious ways had used the adversity to bring me to the next place He apparently wants me. Right now I see the adversity of losing a job in my fifties, which scares some men to death, as another *pele*—a mystery too wondrous to fully understand.

But as great as these *pele*-experiences can be, I well know there are complicating factors. Often the psalmist prayed, "Why, O Lord, do you stand far off? Why do you hide yourself in times of trouble?" (Psalm 10:1).

This kind of prayer raises the long-standing difficulty of how to understand the "hiding of the face" (*tastir panah*) in Jewish theology. Throughout the Psalter, writers confess this experience of God's real *absence* from their lives (13:1; 30:7; 44:24; 69:17; 88:14; 102:2). No phrase better captures the inner feelings of the sufferer under trial than this "hiding of the face."

Is this "hiding" a real absence of God's presence from

the life of the believer? Or is it just that man *perceives* God as absent? This is hotly debated. God himself has decreed that He would turn His face away from His people when they did not pursue His ways (Deuteronomy 31:17; 32:20). So Scripture confirms the reality of experiencing God's absence.

Whatever our temporary dismay at waking up to find all sense of God gone from our souls. God's silence is not permanent. God *does* speak in the worst of human disasters, diseases, and difficulties. Job's only request was for God to speak to him and affirm his innocence or show him where his sin was (Job 10:1–2; 13:3; 31:35). Job got his request! But when God speaks He speaks strangely in the violence of a storm (38:1) and not in the small, still voice which Elijah heard (1 Kings 19:12). When God speaks He answers, "I will question you, and you shall answer me"! (Job 38:3; 40:7). Following this statement, God asks Job over seventy questions, covering everything from how a child is formed in its mother's womb, to how a man might capture the uncontrollable Leviathan!

I conclude from Job's experience that God does indeed speak to us in adversity, but not always in ways we desire or seek. We want answers from God, but He provides questions . . . lots of them. Therefore, the mystery of what God is doing in adversity lies more in the kind of issues God is asking us to face than in trying to figure out what the specific meaning of the adversity is. Job never found out the reason for his suffering. God instead provided him seventy questions to ponder, and all of them reveal the transcendent greatness of God.

In pondering, then, God can cause us to get more in touch with who we are as men. We also get a frontal reminder—equivalent to a blow on the head—of who God is! As one of my professors once said, "Why does a dog have fleas?'' Answer: ''To remind him that he is a dog and not a man.'' Perhaps, that's part of the divine view of adversity. Pain, suffering, and difficulty reaffirm the God/man distinction. It shows me who God is and who I am.

With a divine perspective on adversity I believe we can see how inadequate our human assumptive worldview is. My picture of reality is not painted correctly, and the frame is not nearly large enough. If we accept adversity as the deserved judgment on the fallen race, we cannot hold to the naive assumption that we are immune from suffering. *To be human is to be very vulnerable.*

Likewise, if adversity is rooted in the mysterious interworkings between God and Satan, why should we expect everything to make sense and be just and fair? Since Satan is alive and well on planet earth, injustice should never surprise us. If God is free to do whatever He pleases and not disclose His specific purposes to us, then why should we seek a clear rationale for His actions?

Is it not better to fall on our face in humility and chalk up the experience to one of His wondrous mysteries unfolding before us?

Beyond Myself

As a man, then, I need a competency outside of myself—an adequacy that can never be taken away. It is only God's gracious adequacy that allows me to accept and enjoy the mysterious aspects of adversity (2 Corinthians 9:8; 12:8–10). In short, I contend the biblical picture of reality is better suited for understanding and enduring adversity, and thus much harder to shatter when adversity strikes.

Christ provides the adequacy men need to survive and thrive in adversity. And so it's crucial to see how Christ can be our model for enduring hardship and remaining faithful under trial . . . while we await the wonders of God as they slowly unfold.

For Thought and Discussion

1. Reflect upon your most recent "trial." Did you try to see what meaning there might be in the trial? Were you questioning God or listening for His voice? From your current perspective, what might have God been asking of you?
2. Have you tried to understand the impossible or incomprehensible? As a man, do you find it difficult to enjoy things you can't understand? Think of some area where you have enjoyed the benefits of mystery.
3. Have you experienced an extraordinary work of God in the midst of adversity? Recall it, and thank God for the experience.

Notes

1. Quoted in Dennis Wholey, *When the Worst That Can Happen Already Has* (New York: Berkley Publishing, 1993), p. 105.
2. W. Schnieder, C. Brown, quoting B. Gerhardsson in *Dictionary of the New Testament*, Vol. 3, p. 800.
3. Ibid., pp. 798–811.
4. R. Laird Harris, et al., *Theological Wordbook of the Old Testament*, Vol. 2 (Chicago: Moody Press, 1980), p. 723.

CHRIST . . . Who Suffers With Us

In my experience, adversity prompts one of two opposite reactions in men. Some men rage at God and shake their fists at Him for "ruining" their lives—while other guys are prompted to draw nearer to God. They find in their pain a larger perspective of God and a more enlightened view of themselves.

The irony is that both men end up speaking to the same God . . . one in anger, the other in humble submission.

In the last chapter, I tried to provide a more biblical worldview for men enduring trials. What we need to see now is the role Jesus, our brother, plays in our pain and struggles. If adversity humbles us by breaking down our ill-conceived assumptions about life, then we desperately need someone who has gone before to show us the humble submission to God that leads us through the pain. Thankfully, Jesus is "the Way"—not only to God, but also through the pain we are in.

On Holy Ground

Those who take pilgrimages to Israel anticipate walking where Jesus walked. They are often disillusioned to find that many of the historic sites are hotly debated by scholars. Their location is not always certain.

When it comes to Christ's passion, however, the historical sites are a little more certain—the house of the high priest, Caiaphas, where Jesus was first interrogated, then mocked and fist-beaten by Caiaphas' guards; the Antonia Fortress, where Pontius Pilate, the Roman procurator, stayed; and the Roman barracks where Jesus was beaten, scourged, crowned with thorns, until He was a bloody, broken victim.

I've had very few emotional experiences during my several trips to Israel, but I must confess at these two sites of Jesus' suffering I feel a certain unexplainable connection to my Lord. At both places I feel I am on "holy ground." Here Jesus was beaten, whipped, spat upon, mocked, and dragged off for execution as a criminal—and it's here I sense His suffering on my behalf. The stones below my feet could be the red-stained stones upon which my Savior's blood flowed.

I am glad these sites exist because they represent for me the intense struggle Christ went through on behalf of the world. We have in Jesus a man who endured adversity. In this sense, Jesus' human life provides us with a visual model of how we, too, can handle our own warfare.

The imitation of Christ is one of the most long-standing practices of the spiritual life.[1] Unfortunately, it has come to stand more at the heart of Catholic spirituality than some of the more evangelical approaches.[2] The Reformers generally focused more on the Pauline doctrine of our grafted-in, completed union with Christ, while placing less emphasis on the struggle and journey of growing in the life of Christ.

In this chapter, I hope to show how both the example of Christ and a dynamic living union with Christ are essential components in surviving trials. We don't read very far in the Gospel accounts until we find Jesus facing difficulty. Even His entry into the earthly scene was anything but easy. Immediately after His birth, Jesus' life was threatened by Herod's sword, causing His young parents to flee to Egypt (Matthew 2:14–15).

As an adult, Jesus is led by the Spirit into the wilderness to be tested by the devil (Matthew 4:1). This wilderness temptation provides us with one of the most illuminating accounts of how we can defeat diabolical adversities in our lives.

Testing

The entire temptation scene recalls the divine testing of Israel as God's son in the wilderness (Deuteronomy 6–8), and the time when they were taught how to be totally dependent upon God because of their weakened state. Jesus, going without food for forty days, is left in a completely weakened position before His tempter. And Satan attacks at the point of Jesus' greatest weakness. "Turn these stones into bread," he tempts. Jesus counters by quoting Deuteronomy 8:3, underscoring the reality that man must live by what comes out of the mouth of God, not by what life gives him or denies him.

Having been defeated on the provision issue, Satan then moves the temptation to the realm of *divine protection*. Placing Jesus on the pinnacle of the holy city, Satan quotes Psalm 91:11–12, and asks Jesus to jump. Satan knew this passage, in context, has to do with God's sovereign protection for our *souls*. To the spirit of man, God is a shelter (v. 1), a refuge (vv. 2, 9) and a fortress (v. 2). Jesus again counters by quoting Deuteronomy 6:16, "Do not test the Lord your God." Jesus makes it clear that just because God is sovereign, it doesn't mean men should jump off buildings to prove it. This is tantamount to testing God, which is a *violation* of the Deuteronomy passage.

Satan, being defeated again, moves the scene to a high mountain. Here, he shows Jesus the kingdoms of the world (Matthew 4:8), and offers all the earthly real estate in return for Jesus' allegiance and worship. Jesus responds to Satan by quoting the next verse in this Deuteronomy passage, "Fear the Lord your God, serve him only" (6:13). The point is clear. Where Israel, God's "firstborn," had succumbed to the temptations inherent in earthly properties, Jesus the unique Son of God overcame it. His means was by quoting God's own words.

In the three critical areas where we men often fail, Jesus prevailed—and He won in a way we can emulate.

How many men have believed the deceptive idea that we—with our strengths, skills, and drive—can adequately protect and provide for ourselves and our family . . . without God? We look to adequate life insurance coverage for our protection and our employers for job security. We feel our protection and provision needs will be met by good financial planning or finding the right job with good benefits. These are all valuable resources, but when we begin to place our explicit trust in them, we have made them into false gods. We have believed the lie of Satan and lost an important round of temptation with the Evil One.

Men are also caught in the temptation to trust in property. I have known several men who lost their shirts in "big property" deals. Again, real estate is a wonderful asset. But when we believe the lie that property, and the financial lev-

erage that comes from it, can make our lives more prosperous or secure—I wonder how much we end up trapped and
hurt by Satan's lies.

When these false securities fail us, we can look to Jesus
as the man who withstood temptations by remaining dependent upon God and His Word. In rejecting these temptations, Jesus defeated Satan as a flesh-and-blood human
being without any supernatural aid. His only weapon, as a
vulnerable human, was the Word of God.

Is there a lesson here?

Throughout His life, Jesus would face adversity—from
demon powers, foolish disciples, betraying "friends," the
religious establishment, and the Roman "military police."
And in His final hours He was left alone, with no attorney,
no friends, and no family to comfort or defend Him. From
the human perspective, He died a broken, battered criminal.

Because of all this adversity, Christ is truly a sympa-
thetic high priest. He truly knows our feelings of victimization, betrayal, humiliation, and abandonment.

When I face adversity, I know I have in Christ a mentor
who has gone before me—has felt what I feel, and who came
out on the other side victorious. From His life I learn how
to use Scripture to defeat the devices of Satan. I see how He
engaged His enemies, never turning away from them, nor
letting them get to Him. I see how He genuinely loved the
ones who conspired to kill Him—while at the same time,
He never rolled over and played dead in regard to their intentions. He defended and warned His disciples about the
Pharisees and chief priests. He called these dignitaries
some pretty pointed names and stood His ground in dia-
logues with them. Even during Jesus' mock trial we see that
He is more in charge than the authorities (see John 19:11).

Even though everything was against Jesus, He didn't act like a victim!

From studying Jesus' example in adversity, I learn I don't have to suffer character assassination without defending my integrity, assuming it's more spiritual to merely "keep quiet." Jesus certainly did not keep quiet when His character was questioned. (See 1 Peter 4:1; 2:21–25.)

But there is also a more exciting aspect to Christ's role in our adversity. Our adversity is experienced by the living Christ as a continuation of His suffering.

Living Union With Christ

Jesus affirmed for His disciples the permanence of His relationship with them. He said, "I will be with you always, to the very end of the age" (Matthew 28:20). The writer of the Hebrews reaffirmed the commitment of God to His people, "Never will I leave you; never will I forsake you" (Hebrews 13:5). On their last night together, Jesus taught His disciples the unique relationship they would have with Him through the Holy Spirit who was to come. "On that day you will realize that I am in my Father, and you are in me, and I am in you" (John 14:20).

To be "in Christ" means that I am really, actually alive in the personal experience of Christ. The promise of His indwelling presence is not just a legal description of my standing before God, but a living experiential reality. Christ's real presence is in me, and I am in Him.

Jesus' promise that we could have the Spirit of God living with us—and *in* us—is what drove the Jewish religious leaders crazy. Jesus told them one Sabbath day, a day when no work was to be done, that His Father was still working (present tense) and that He himself was also working (present tense) (John 5:17). God's work did not end with His Sabbath rest at the end of creation but continued to that very day. Likewise, the Father's work was being continued in the experience and ministry of Jesus.

A further example is found in the Pauline teaching that what God is doing in the world He is doing in the life of the believer. That is to say, what I am doing when I submit myself to God, Christ is doing. How else can we understand Paul's statement in Philippians 2:13: "For it is God who works *in you* to will and to act according to his good purpose"? In this spiritual union, God and the believer are *together* accomplishing God's good purpose in the world.

If Christ has a genuine presence in my life, He is never separated from what's happening to me. If He is truly in my life, He is intimately aware of my pain and suffers with me in my misfortune.

Unfortunately, many believers are only taught about Christ's work of redemption and suffering as it relates to the initial act of salvation. Through His one sacrifice, we are made holy once and for all (Hebrews 10:10). But Jesus' Upper Room teaching told about the One who would be sent to our side—"the Comforter" (John 13–17). And Paul's understanding of our "sonship" was that we are birthed by the Spirit (Romans 8:16). And John said, "We know that we live in him and he in us, because he has given us of his Spirit" (1 John 4:13). All this says that the Spirit of Christ *really* indwells us and God is *really* at work in what we are doing . . . and in what we are struggling through.

The point is this: Just as God felt the pain and suffering of His people in Egypt (Exodus 2:24; 3:7), so Jesus feels the pain of His brothers. This intimate connection between Jesus and us, His body, has been written off by some as "just a lot of human language about God." The implication being that God does not really feel, grieve, or hurt with His people. This view leaves us with a non-passionate, incapable-

of-truly-feeling kind of deity. Unfortunately, many believers have had this teaching distort their thinking about
Jesus. In response to this assive and distant view of God,
scholar John Stott writes,

> It is true that Old Testament language is an accom-
> modation to our human understanding, and that God is
> represented as experiencing human emotion. Yet, to
> acknowledge that His feelings are not human is not to
> deny that they are real. If they are only metaphorical,
> then the only God left to us will be the infinite iceberg
> of metaphysics. . . . The frequent anthropopathisms
> (which ascribe human suffering to God) are not to be
> rejected as crude or primitive, but rather to be wel-
> comed as crucial to our understanding of him.[3]

In the final analysis, it comes down to this: If God is not
really present in our suffering, then He is not really present
at all. He is a dispassionate, absent deity. But that's not the
case. The psalmist expressed his wonder that there is no
place in heaven or in the depths of hell (*sheol* and darkness) where God's presence could be absent (Psalm 139:7–
16).

Applications abound from the real-presence union with
Christ we can enjoy.

My friend who was in Vietnam blurted out, "Christ
could not have been in Nam." Even though he was a Christian at the time and knew his Bible, emotionally he had
come to the conclusion that Jesus could not have been present during the fire fights or their "gook parties."

I tried to explain my understanding. "Jesus was there in
Vietnam. When your buddy had his legs blown off by a hidden mine, Jesus was there. The one who bled on the cross
knows what your friend felt as he lay there bleeding to
death. He felt the same anguish and anger you felt. When

you cut off body parts from dead Viet Cong in rage and re-taliation, Jesus was violently grieved at having His own image marred and mutilated. But knowing fully what happened on both sides of the DMZ, He still went to the cross to forgive such atrocities."

My friend just kept looking at me in utter amazement. He finally wiped a tear from his eye and just kept repeating, "Jesus was really there . . . Jesus was really there? I can't believe it!"

The sad spectacle is this: We mortal men think we can block God out of horror, suffering, pain, and loss with the force of our unbelief. Because our hearts respond with numbness or grief or anger and we cannot sense Him, we say He isn't there. This is unwitting arrogance.

Whatever adversity we have faced or will face, Jesus *is* there experiencing the pain along with us. He was and continues to be a man of sorrows, very much at home with our grief. Because He is our attorney (advocate), He is always turned toward the Father, reminding Him of the atoning sacrifice He made for us (1 John 2:1–2). Knowing that Jesus is there in the midst and depths of my pain is a terribly reassuring and comforting thought. The pains we experience as men should not come as any surprise to us, because Jesus fully revealed the cost in pain which the disciple following Him will experience.

Christ's Instruction About Adversity: Yokes, Crosses, and Thorns

The Pharisees had placed so many impossible regulations upon their followers, there was no way a disciple could ever find rest for his soul. Jesus exposed the heavy weight of the Pharisaic yoke in saying, "They tie up heavy loads and put them on men's shoulders" (Matthew 23:4). In contrast, the discipleship yoke Jesus promises is one of rest. For all who are weary and burdened (probably an illusion to the heavy Pharisaic yoke of religious works), Jesus promises rest for the soul (Matthew 11:28–30). The early church father Clement of Rome called this yoke a "yoke of grace." This is our beginning point for understanding the teaching of Christ. As believers, we are not in an adversarial relationship with Him. Our relationship is a gracious one where we can find peace for our souls even in hardship.

Immediately after Jesus had called His disciples, He gave them a large dose of His reality about their mission. He told them to expect opposition and adversity from both the religious and political communities (Matthew 10:16–20). In this sense, they were to view themselves as "sheep among wolves." Likewise, they should expect opposition from the members of their own households (10:35–37). In the face of adversity, Jesus says, the disciple must "take up his cross and follow me" (10:38).

The apostle Paul labeled the adversity he faced as a "thorn" (2 Corinthians 12:7). He went to God on three occasions and asked for the pain—whatever it was—to be removed (2 Corinthians 12:8).

Paraphrasing God's answer, He returned, "Paul, I have some good news and some bad news for you. Which do you want first?" Paul responds, "Well, let's get the bad news over first. What is it?" God says, "I'm not going to heal you . . . I'm not going to take away your pain." What a blow for this rugged, masculine missionary. God would not take away the pain from his life. Paul probably responded, "Well, then, what is the good news?"

God answered, "My grace is sufficient for you, for my power is made perfect in weakness" (12:9).

Adversities are thorns that penetrate our souls and cause extreme pain. As men, our natural reaction is to fight the pain, deny the pain, or deaden it with some kind of activity, spirituality, or self-medication.

Get ready—this will be tough for some of you: I believe the reality Jesus wants us to face—the reality He prepared His disciples for—was that pain has a work to do in us, and that this work be accepted and welcomed. Why? Because it is only through the work of pain that we truly experience the grace of Christ as our sufficiency.

Once Paul realized this he uttered, "That is why, for Christ's sake, I delight in weaknesses, in insults, in hardships, in persecutions, in difficulties. For when I am weak, then I am strong" (12:10).

I am not sure Christian men today really believe this. Our macho identities are so attuned and driven to winning at all cost, while failure is our worst fear. The belief that we are actually the strongest when we are the weakest is a foreign concept to most of us males.

Christ modeled this strength-in-weakness in His own life. And He has not left us to walk through adversity alone. He promised He would be with us and in us through His indwelling Spirit.

Christ never "hides His face" from the one going through adversity. He is there every step of the way . . . with you.

For Thought and Discussion

1. As men we see ourselves as providers and protectors. We feel we have finally "made it" when we can own property. It was in these three areas that Jesus was tempted. How have you been tempted in the areas of being a good provider or protector? How about the real es-

tate issue? Do you find any temptations here?

2. Have you suffered adversity for your Christian convictions? Did the opposition come from the religious or nonreligious? Does being conformed to the image of Christ mean not being conformed to the "Christian community"?

3. Do you believe Christ actually suffers when you suffer? If so, what is Jesus feeling right now in relation to your life?

Notes

1. See *Christian Spirituality: Five Views of Sanctification*, edited by Donald Alexander (Downers Grove, Ill.: InterVarsity Press, 1988), article by Sinclair B. Ferguson, "The Reformed View," p. 66.

2. In Catholic theology they "imitate" the way of the Cross both in Jerusalem and in their churches by praying through the fourteen stations of the Cross. In the Old City, the via dolorosa.

3. John R. Stott, *The Cross of Christ* (Downers Grove, Ill.: InterVarsity Press, 1986), p. 331.

Attacking Adversity

Sometimes Christianity is viewed as a passive religion for wimps. Critics quote "turn the other cheek" as the pure essence of what Christianity is about. Therefore, to defend yourself, challenge someone, or go on the offensive are seen as incompatible with the teaching of Jesus.

Jesus was anything but passive. I contend the Christian life is intensively active as focused by the hundreds of imperatives found throughout the New Testament. You cannot be an obedient Christian and maintain a couch-potato view of life.

During my early years as a Christian, though, I was deeply confused about this tension between activism and passivism. I felt whatever God was going to do, He'd do it apart from my activity. Therefore, whether it was buying a home or looking for a job, I felt I shouldn't do these things unless God sort of dropped them in my lap. I thought this was the spiritual thing to do based on my biblical understanding of God's Providence. But God used two unrelated events in my life to change the course of my thinking.

When I was a young air force officer attending officer's school, a woman major gave us a briefing on promotion procedures. At that point in my life, I'd had enough experience in the banking business and the ministry to realize it was often the "jerk" who got the promotion, while the well-deserving person was passed over. The major concluded her presentation by saying, "The only person who can get you promoted is *you*. In the air force you have to take charge of your life."

For some reason, this hit me like Jesus confronting Saul on the Damascus road. I had memorized the verse, "For promotion cometh neither from the east, nor from the west, nor from the south. But God is the promoter [actually judge]: he putteth down one and setteth up another" (Psalm 75:6–7, KJV). I had reasoned, "If this psalm is true, then I don't have to do anything to get promoted. God will promote me supernaturally." But my experience said otherwise. I had seen worthy Christian workers passed over, and now this "secular" air force major was telling me it was my responsibility. What a jolt to my worldview!

About this time I read one of my wife's books entitled *A Slow and Certain Light* by Elisabeth Elliot. In her section on the "Means of God's Guidance," a new concept leaped out at me. It was her concept of simple "duty." She writes,

> We are going along in life, doing the usual things, when suddenly we come up against a thing we are not sure about. We need guidance. The temptation is to stop everything and ask for a sign . . . "do the next thing" is one of the best pieces of advice I have ever had. It works in any kind of situation, and is especially helpful when we don't know what to do . . . when some duty lies on our doorstep. The rule is "do it." The doing of that thing may open our eyes to the next.[1]

"Doing the next thing" is a practical next step until a clearer, more objective redirection comes. On the human side, we must be responsible to take charge of our lives and actively take up our biblical responsibilities.

This view of *responsibility* applies equally to adversity. Adversity is something we can attack and manage, even when it causes us to be and feel out of control.

The suggestions on dealing with adversity that form this chapter come from fellow sufferers and "wounded healers"—men whose pain, turned over to God, has helped countless others. The wisdom gained through tough experience will shed light on how you and I can survive the worst of adversity.

Allow Yourself to Feel the Pain

Job was one honest character. He vented to everybody— his friends, God. He openly admitted his "bitterness of soul" (3:20; 7:11; 10:1), "despair" (6:14), "fears" (7:14; 9:34), and "tears" (16:16, 20). Job's "venting" has been found by counselors to be one of the most therapeutic things a man can do with his feelings.

Navy Seals are thought of in the military community as the toughest of the tough, the créme of the special forces. But they are called on to do other things than just military operations. They are sometimes called in on special civilian assignments.

When an Air Florida flight crashed in the Potomac River after leaving Washington National Airport, it was the Navy Seals who were called on to do their well-honed diving routine. Since the plane rapidly descended in the dark icy waters, very few passengers survived. Most were immediately trapped in the flooded jetliner, never escaping their seats. During the long night of bringing up bodies, these "toughest of the tough" Seals were having difficulties.

Their difficulty was certainly not on the operation side, but with their emotions. Chaplains were brought in and tents erected on the banks of the river. When a Seal emerged out of the murky waters with another body, he would go into the Chaplain's tent and, over a cup of warm coffee, unload what he was seeing and feeling.

One Navy Sprint team member recalled, "In the darkness of the river—not being able to see more than one foot in front of your face—suddenly there would be a body right in front of you. It was a freaky, eerie experience and caused us all to freak out." These tough Seals, having been brought into a warm caring environment, were allowed to be human in an inhuman operation and grieve over what they had seen.[2]

Why? Because what they faced at the bottom of the Potomac was far more than the bodies of victims. They were also confronted with the reality that they were very human. All their special forces training, which teaches them to separate feelings from their operational task, could not block out the powerful emotions they were feeling. They too had wives, sons and daughters, mothers and fathers, brothers and sisters, and the shock of remembering them when bringing up these frozen bodies could not be masked or denied. The associations between the dead and the living were too great.

Psychic pain, like physical pain, was created by God. Its function is to let me know that something is wrong—and remind me that I am not God. So it raises the question, "What should I do with pain, once I get in contact with it?"

Reveal Your Wounds to Others

Once we men realize we're in pain (not necessarily a quick process!), the next best thing we can do is to communicate what we're feeling to someone else. Again, this is not easy for men to do. We would rather keep up the appearance of our "all-togetherness" and just pretend in front of our friends and loved ones that we are *okay*. But this is not healthy.

A Harvard University researcher says, "People in crisis who tend by nature to keep their innermost feelings to themselves release hormones that lower their immune system's resistance to disease."[3] Other research has shown a vital relationship between the strength of our social support systems and our emotional and physical resilience under severe stress. Psychologist James Pennebaker studied more than 2,000 people who had suffered trauma, loss of life, rape, and physical abuse. He found if they managed to confide in at least one person about the event, they developed far less incidence of illnesses, covering everything from headaches to lung disease![4] A National Institute of Mental Health report concluded that many of our normal daily conversations are in reality mutual "counseling sessions," whereby we exchange the reassurance and advice that help us deal with routine stresses.[5]

A caution. As I alluded earlier, I have found it difficult to open my inner life to most men. The reason is simple. It takes a trusted relationship, in which feelings can be openly shared. Among men, these relationships are often rare. In addition, we fear if we open up with someone we will be seen as weak, unworthy, or unspiritual.

This is what Job faced with his friends. Apparently, they were more concerned about the correctness of Job's theology (and their own) than about him as a person. On more than one occasion they attributed the cause of his suffering to some hidden sin (4:8–11; 11:13–14). It was Job's true friend Elihu who defended Job's innocence and backed off the others for speaking wrongly about Job (32:1–5). Elihu

was the kind of friend Job needed to support his feelings
and get the other pathetic "counselors" off his back.

I am of the persuasion that most men who go through a
hard time do not need professional counseling or an official
support group. But we do need at least one human being
who can listen to us, affirm that our pain is legitimate, and
provide some insight *without trying to quick-fix the pain.*
Whether it's your spouse, a friend, pastor, or counselor, the
important thing is to have someone to lay our "stuff" on as
men.

Another important way we can attack adversity is by
finding something to do with our pain.

Do Something . . . With Your Pain

As men it's a scary thing to realize there is nothing we
can do to change a situation.

Here again, researchers have found those who do best
in the worst kind of adversity are those who *take some kind
of action* in spite of their loss of control. Though we may
feel powerless in the situation, there are usually some
things we can do to help us through. Many men, however,
remain stuck in self-pity, feeling so victimized by the situation they think they are powerless to make any decisions
or initiate any action. What action does in the face of adversity is to take us out of ourselves. It lets us interact with
other people and begin to move toward some goal. I know,
because I've been there.

I once went through a time when I was so paralyzed by
fear because of an adverse situation, I went to my office
every day (at least I got out of the house) and told my sec-
retary to hold all calls. I then put my head down on the desk
and went to sleep. I was so depressed by thinking I had ruined my family's lives by moving to a new part of the coun-

try and then having everything fall apart that I couldn't really function. I was immobilized by fear, angry at God for allowing this to happen, and frustrated with my wife and family for blaming me for the move.

When my head was off the desk, though, I began almost unconsciously to scribble out lists of how difficult my life was. I wondered if other men's lives were the same. I took a straw poll at a men's Bible study by asking them to comment on my list of issues. I found out these guys struggled with the same kind of feelings.

From the growing list of uneasiness I saw in my own life and the lives of other men, I began writing about the issues I saw emerging over and over again. Little did I know that what I was doing was journaling my pain and interacting about it with other men. My journal became my first published work, *Uneasy Manhood*, and launched my writing career.

What happened through the first small steps was that I regained the lost sense of control over my life. Seeing myself as powerless, I became a slave to my feelings of impotence, and had I remained that way the results would have been devastating. Sickness reigns supreme on the extremes of overcontrol and undercontrol. In order to survive adversity—which removes our sense of control—we must take back some of the ground of our lives. Clinically, this is called *"regaining the focus of control."*

Because this concept is sometimes debated by Christians as not being found in the Bible, let me offer a biblical perspective.

Stewardship of Our Lives

As human beings made in God's image, I believe we have been given the stewardship of our environment (Genesis 1:26). The idea of stewardship involves control. What this means is we have a deep-seated compulsion to rule the environment around us. The original design was for us to rule in wisdom, benevolence, and equity. When sin entered the world, this divine design was corrupted. Now obsessive-compulsives rule too much, and dysfunctionals too little.

Adversity makes even the best of people unable to function for a while. When this happens we need a sphere over which we can regain some control. We may not be able to control everything. No one ever can. But for our own mental health, we need to regain the control of *something*. We do this by taking action.

Is control of self a biblical doctrine? For me this is an absurd question with an obvious answer. In the Greek world, "self-control," *enkrateia*, meant literally to be "empowered." Socrates thought it was one of the chief virtues. In the New Testament, *enkrateia*, "self-control," never takes on the stoic idea of an ascetic ideal but certainly the idea of "renunciation . . . of something that stands in the way of following Jesus."[6] To *renounce* something requires a certain control over one's self or will.

In the marital area, for instance, Satan can tempt a man for his lack of *enkrateia* in regard to his wife (1 Corinthians 7:6).

When a man does not cultivate a sexual relationship with his wife, his ability to control himself sexually is diminished, and he becomes open to outside influences. Paul also views the lack of *enkrateia* as one of the characteristic signs of the end times (2 Timothy 3:3) and sees "self-control" as one of the critical virtues for consideration of an elder (Titus 1:8). Peter also sees *enkrateia* as a supreme character virtue (2 Peter 1:6). Finally, Paul attributes this positive character trait as being the by-product of the Holy

Spirit's work in the believer's life (Galatians 5:23).

I have to conclude that Spirit-led control has vital importance to both the biblical writers and to recovering our footing when turmoil hits. Much in our life may be out of control, but we can always control ourselves and to some extent something around us.

Ryan White was one of the first young hemophiliacs to contract the HIV virus through blood transfusions. He made headlines when his mother sued the local school board for not allowing Ryan to continue in school. Her action was in response to little Ryan's desire to attack his situation vigorously. First, he wanted a dog, and he didn't want anyone else to care for it or feed it. Next, he wanted a paper route. Everyone thought, *There's no way he can do these things.* But he did. Finally, after growing sick of watching television all day, he wanted to go back to school. This is when the community drew the line. Other parents were fearful of Ryan infecting their children. Ryan's mother sued—not for the money, but for the opportunity for Ryan to regain some control of his life.

They won, and Ryan stayed in school.[7]

Lack of action just leads to depression, which keeps us immobile.

Sometimes doing something with our pain is as simple as shaving. Ambassador Bruce Laingren made sure he shaved every day during his 404-day captivity in Iran. He admitted, "The daily practice was critical . . . it helped preserve my fading self-image."[8] For POWs, control was a simple, self-imposed exercise routine done in the limited confines of their cells. General Dozier, the American NATO Army commander in Italy, when captured by the Italian Red Guard, was blindfolded, handcuffed to his bed, with blaring rock music being played on a radio headset covering his ears. Even in this condition, he tried to control what he could control. He said he looked forward to the one time during the day when his captors released him, then fed and interrogated him. At least, it was human contact. So during his periods of complete immobility, he mentally geared up for this time with his captors. He put together in his mind the merits of capitalism over and against the failures of communism, and reflected back on all his education about democracy, so that during his interrogations he was more in charge than they were![9]

Attacking adversity requires taking some initial steps. They don't have to be gigantic ones. Even the smallest of steps—like shaving—gets us moving and out of ourselves. And tomorrow we can go even further.

Once we have started to do something with our pain, giving this movement some specific definition can also be very helpful.

Reaching Out

One of the worst—and most *miraculous*—experiences of my life came in an agonizing meeting with a couple and their expert physician. As their pastor, I was there to be a part of the process of making the most difficult decision one can ever make ... deciding to withdraw the means by which a young child is being kept alive. In this case, all brain activity had ceased, but a respirator was keeping their child "alive."

In the middle of the neurologist's summary of various tests, the mother noticed the physician was having a difficult time retaining his doctorly composure. I watched, amazed, as she reached across the table, put her hand on his, and said, "You're having a difficult time with this, aren't you?"

I could not believe what I was seeing. Here, the grieving

mother of this brain-dead child was reaching out to the professional, who could no longer keep his pain hidden. What was I here for?

Researchers again have observed the power of "reaching out." One of the greatest things we can do to get us through our own turmoil is to offer even the smallest bit of help to others. In the act of helping someone else, healing takes place in us. It is so commonplace that we fail to recognize the principle.

Paul writes to the church of Corinth,

> Praise be to the God and Father of our Lord Jesus Christ, the Father of compassion and the God of all comfort, who comforts us in all our troubles, so that we can comfort those in any trouble with the comfort we ourselves have received from God. For just as the sufferings of Christ flow over into our lives, so also through Christ our comfort overflows (2 Corinthians 1:3–4).

As we experience God's comfort in our difficulties, one of the meaningful things we can do with the experience is to take this comfort to others. Sometimes in comforting others, we find the needed comfort of God for ourselves. The pain created by adversity mysteriously becomes more bearable when we take on a mission to comfort others. Someone once said, "Ugly facts challenge us to beautify them." To survive adversity, perhaps it is our challenge to turn outward and in some way beautify the lives of others.

In reaching out to someone, we begin to find meaning in what happened to us—and perhaps gain a little perspective as to why God allowed the adversity to happen. God comforts us in our affliction *in order that* we might be the agents of comfort for others.

Can you imagine what it must have been like to have

received a phone call telling you as a parent that your son had just shot someone. Then you learn the identity of the person he shot . . . the President of the United States. That's exactly what happened to Jack Hinckley. In the following months after his son, John, had shot President Reagan, Jack left his comfortable Colorado home and business, moved to McLean, Virginia, where he could be near his son, and started the American Mental Health Fund. In his own words, "I decided to try to cause something good to come from John's illness and tragedy."[10]

Knowingly or not, men like Jack Hinckley are doing the most productive thing they can do to enhance their own recovery from such adversity. The unemployment ministry in my own church is headed by such a man. After being unemployed for a year, he decided he would call a meeting of all other unemployed people every Monday night. This turned into a part support group, part resume-writing time. The Monday evening time together gradually grew into a whole seminar that several in the group presented to the church. When people in the larger community learned about the seminar, they asked if it could be presented at other places. Today, this outreach has not only given many men and women the kind of hope and support they needed during a difficult time, but it has also become a resource pool for employers looking for personnel. Perhaps Shakespeare had it right: "Draw from the heart of suffering a means of inspiration and survival."

Christians face a unique struggle in adversity simply because they wrestle with both the adversity and with God. Therefore, believers at some point need to listen for God's voice.

God's Voice Is in the Pain

Like Job, we all want God to speak to *us* during times of deep trial. But if God *is* speaking to me, how can I know for sure what the message is? Or if God seems silent, how do I interpret this silence?

One way to know what God may be saying is to start with Scripture. We hear God's voice in the divinely breathed Word, which teaches, rebukes, corrects, and trains us in righteousness (2 Timothy 3:16). Peter told us we would do well to pay attention to the words of the prophets, since they have their origin not in men but in God (2 Peter 1:19–21). As Christians, we are also indwelt by the Holy Spirit of God, and so we have a Helper in our own heart. It is the Spirit who "speaks in groanings," and intercedes according to God's will, when we do not know how to pray (Roman 8:26–27). This provides us with "one who speaks," when *we* do not how to speak.[11] When we read Scripture, it is this benevolent Spirit that bears witness to the words of God and makes the thoughts of God known in our hearts. "And he who searches our hearts knows the mind of the Spirit," and, "We have . . . received the Spirit who is from God, that we may understand what God has freely given us" (Romans 8:27; Corinthians 2:12).

We find God's voice in Scripture can come through the voices of others. David cries out, "Why, O Lord, do you stand far off? Why do you hide yourself in times of trouble?" (Psalm 10:1). "Repay the wicked for their deeds and for their evil work" (Psalm 28:4). Listening to him I have the assurance that human emotions are not "unspiritual" responses for the believer. They are, in fact, the experiences of "a man after God's own heart." These are God's words coming to me from a fellow sufferer's life. When Solomon concludes life is just "chasing after the wind" (Ecclesiastes 1:14), I find comfort in knowing his experience is no different than mine on many occasions and—more importantly—that his feelings of futility are not outside the range of God's love. As the divine author God spoke these words through Solomon's observation and understanding of life.

I still remember how God used that well-worn verse—
Romans 8:28—in my own life during a particular adversity.
I had often claimed this verse as my assurance that no mat-
ter what happened, I knew God was "working everything
in accordance with his will." But during a painful experi-
ence of unemployment, as I was meditating on the passage,
God seemed to highlight the phrase "to them that love
God."

A frightening new insight struck my mind. "All things
don't *necessarily* work together for good. This is only the
experience of those who truly love God." My favorite verse
on the sovereignty of God suddenly became a threat. What
the verse did in that instant was to focus me on my responsibility and reaction to the adversity I was facing. *If I did
not truly love God, I would never be able to see what God
was doing in my life. I could not see how all things were
working together for good!*[12]

Another way we can hear God's voice is in *prayer*. As
noted in the life of Job, the way in which God finally answered Job was not by giving reasons for his suffering *but
by asking Job questions*!

In our prayers, I believe we need to do more listening
than talking. Most of us dump our gut prayers before God
pretty quickly. He knows what's going on in the depths of
our hearts, so there's no kidding Him about our feelings
anyway. He knows if we're ticked off, depressed, angry at
life, or mad at Him. These are our true-to-life, manly
prayers. But having prayed, then comes the time for listening.

Let me be clear: We are listening for God's questioning
of us, not His explanations of himself to us. I may *prefer*,
and find more comfort in, listening for God's *"I love you."*
But I may need to hear His questioning of my heart, *"Why*

do you have so much of yourself invested in your work?"

Some men may need to learn to pray the honest prayer of the demoniac's father: "Lord, I believe; help thou mine unbelief" (Mark 9:24, KJV). Adversity can create a certain amount of unbelief, even for the most sincere believer. So this prayer validates the experience of many men in prayer. They believe in Jesus, but their personal experiential belief-system has been so shattered by trials they need help for their unbelief.

Other men may hear God's voice through the liturgy. One friend of mine was going through so many different types of adversity at once, he reached the point where the Scriptures and his own prayers had no real impact on his soul. As he described the way God brought comfort to him, he said, "I went back to the liturgy of my youth. I rediscovered the Episcopal *Book of Common Prayer* and its daily readings from the Psalter. For an entire six months, this was the way God kept in touch with me while I was so out of it I couldn't pray, read the Bible, or do anything. I now have a new appreciation of how God can speak through church liturgy, which I once discounted."

God Walks Into the Depths

God also speaks within the recesses of our hearts as He opens us up through the circumstances of adversity.

David affirmed that, no matter what he faced in terms of adversity, God would be his refuge (Psalm 16:1–4). He then accepted the realities in his life as his *"cup and portion"* (16:5–6). He then praises the Lord who "counsels him" and his own heart who "instructs him" (16:7). In this Hebrew parallelism, the first line affirms it is God who *ya'atz*—that is advises and counsels.[13] God's counsel comes to him *"during the nights, my inward affections and emotions ad-*

monish, instruct and discipline me.''[14] David found God speaking to him through the inward processes of his own heart. God can speak to us in discipline, instruction, and admonishment, by listening to processes of our hearts, too. How so?

As we listen for God's voice—sometimes in the lonely dark of night—we may find our own heart surfacing some *new insight.* We might see how selfish and spoiled we are— or we might be surprised by an element of goodness we thought we never had. Some men find that challenge and pain instruct them about their hidden darker impulses. Through this, all of us can experience a refreshingly new encounter with the gracious redemption of Christ.

As we evaluate the circumstances of our adversity, we might begin to see or hear God's voice. History is always difficult to evaluate, especially when we're in the process of living it! We all claim 20–20 hindsight. But seeing God *in* the circumstance of adversity is not an easy task. How we view what has happened to us is left to our interpretation. We know God is the prime mover of history—but the mere *facts* of history do not provide the reason for the events.[15] If we listen, God can have His say. That is the big *if* that's up to you and me.

When people ask me why we moved from Honolulu to Dallas and then to Philadelphia, I have to plead "temporary insanity." Especially in reference to our Philadelphia move. We prayed about the move, thought it was God's will, and felt a peace about the decision. But within months of arriving at our new ministry, both my wife and I knew we had made a terrible decision. Nothing turned out as we thought. The church board and pastor were terribly divided, staff left, job descriptions were changed, and my kids were unhappy from the start.

What was God saying to me in these circumstances? Ten

years later, I can only tell you that God has used these tough experiences to teach me a lot about myself, about the deception of appearances and promises, about the wicked betrayal that can come from the best of God's children.

I have to conclude that at least one of God's purpose for the adversity was to grow me up a little.

Chalk It Up to Growing

A few years back, I did a study on "biblical maturity." I wanted to find out all the Bible had to say on the subject. I was terribly disappointed! Almost everyone agrees the goal of the Christian life is *Christlikeness*, or being conformed to the image of Christ. But what I was interested in finding out was *how* this Christlikeness could be produced. I had long since burned myself out on all the "list approaches" to the spiritual life. You know—"Do these five things and you will become a mature Christian." My problem was I had done the five things for years and still struggled with the same problems. So I was going back to the drawing board to see what the Bible taught.

I was shocked. I could only find a couple of passages that connected the concept of maturity with something I could do to attain it. The clearest passage was James 1:2–4. Here, clear as could be, was what produced "proven character or maturity." How? By going through *trials*!

James says, "Consider it all joy, my brothers, whenever you face trials of many kinds, because you know that the testing of your faith develops perseverance. Perseverance must finish its work so that you may be mature and complete, not lacking in anything."

What produces maturity? *Adversity. Trials. Putting our faith under extreme tension.* These are the things God uses to grow us up as men. Adversity matures us. Adversity creates within us what our education and parental discipline failed to achieve. In this sense, it is God's good gift. Adversity properly processed, and walked through, results in growth. While groping and searching within ourselves, and debating with the God of the universe, we find a new awareness of both God and ourselves. Self-discovery and insight into God seem to go hand in hand.

Ironically, it's most often through adversity that we find a new mission in life. I would not be writing this book had I not personally experienced the adversities mentioned in these pages. New direction as the leading of God, or simply the desires of the heart, or a new compassion for others are the unexpected results of tragedy and trial.

The apostle Peter knew from personal experience how he had grown through his trial of faith. Having denied his Lord three times—when he'd been warned he would do so!—was the worst failure a man could face. Where was his manly courage in the face of opposition? Where was the *old* Peter, so eager to defend the Messianic cause? Where was the one who had so clearly proclaimed to Jesus, "You are the Christ!" (Matthew 16:13–20). As Jesus had predicted, Satan had sifted Peter's *confession*, his *confidence*, and his *character*—and found it terribly wanting.

But Peter walked it out and learned the lesson in the adversity. He later wrote,

> Now for a little while you may have to suffer grief in all kinds of trials. These have come so that your faith—of greater worth than gold, which perishes even though refined by fire—may be proved genuine and may result in praise, glory and honor when Jesus Christ is revealed (1 Peter 1:6–7).

Adversity—if we bring it under the lordship of Christ—refines us. And it grows us up as men.

For Thought and Discussion

1. What do you think about "doing the next thing" as God's will in adversity? Is it too simple or rational? When facing adversity, do we need something simple to do?
2. What have you learned from the pain you have experienced? Do you think anyone else could be helped by your insights? If not, what else could be done with your lessons from life?
3. Do you have anyone to process your pain and problems with? Do you see the need in your life to share your suffering with someone else, or do you still believe as most men, it is better to just "stuff it," shut up about it, and go it alone?

Notes

1. Elisabeth Elliot, *A Slow and Certain Light* (Waco: Word Publishers, 1973), pp. 87–88.
2. Illustration given by the United States Navy Sprint Team (Rapid Intervention Team) on the role of the Navy Seals in the Air Florida crash, Association of Military Surgeon General's Conference, Las Vegas, November 10, 1987.
3. Research quoted in *Winning Life's Toughest Battles*, p. 19.
4. Ibid., p. 18.
5. Ibid., p. 16.
6. *Dictionary of New Testament Theology*, Vol. 1, Colin Brown, ed. (Grand Rapids: Zondervan, 1977), p. 495.
7. Article by Jeanne White, "The Strength to Fight Comes From Within," in *When the Worst That Can Happen Already Has*, pp. 153–157.
8. *Winning Life's Toughest Battles*, p. 35.
9. Story told by General Dozier at the Armed Forces Communications and Electronics Association banquet, 1988, Philadelphia.

10. *Winning Life's Toughest Battles*, p. 111.
11. On this verse, Scholar John Murray writes, "But that 'we know not what to pray for as we ought' brings to the forefront how helpless we are in our infirmity and lays the basis for the particular kind of help afforded by the Spirit." John Murray, *Epistle to the Romans* (Grand Rapids: Eerdmans, 1968), p. 311.
12. I learned much later that my "divine insight" in that moment was validated by careful exegesis of the passage. Murray suggests, " 'to them that love God' is placed in the position of emphasis and characterizes those to whom the assurance belongs . . . in the benign and all-embracing plan of God the discrete elements all work together for good for them that love God. It is not to be supposed that they have any virtue or efficacy in themselves to work in concrete for this end." Murray, *Epistle to the Romans*, p. 314.
13. See Brown, Driver, Briggs, *Lexicon*, p. 419.
14. Ibid., pp. 415–416.
15. Roy Swanstrom's excellent work, *History in the Making* (Downers Grove, Ill.: InterVarsity Press, 1978), for an excellent Christian evaluation of "secular history."